Guam
Guatemala
Honduras
Hong Kong
The Republic of Ireland
Jordan
Madeira
Malta
The Commonwealth of the Northern Mariana Islands
Monaco
Panama
The Philippines
Portugal
Puerto Rico
St. Kitts and Nevis
Seychelles
Singapore
Turks and Caicos
United Kingdom

Introduction
Why Invest Abroad?

"I sn't the United States still the most stable, free, and prosperous nation on earth? What safer haven could I possibly find for my assets? Where else could I find such a diverse range of investment opportunity?"

Many investors feel unsure about putting some of their money in a foreign country. All things being equal between nations, there really would be no reason to diversify your investments internationally. After all, you know your own country much better than any other. You know your laws, your customs, and the people with whom you deal habitually; whereas foreign customs seem to be strange indeed. If you keep your assets in your own country, it is much easier to keep an eye on them and to get to them rapidly when they are needed.

But all things are not equal between nations. Some currencies are traditionally stronger and more inflation free than others.

Interest rates vary, as do foreign-exchange regulations, banking laws, securities regulations, and political and economic freedom. Therefore, geographical diversification has become necessary for prudent investors of any nationality—even for the Swiss.

Most nations of the world eagerly welcome foreign capital, offering tax advantages and favorable interest and exchange rates to woo investors' capital from other nations.

Sending a portion of your capital outside your own nation requires that you sharpen your awareness of a whole new set of economic and political indicators. Each nation has different regulations, taxes, and exchange restrictions, not to mention the limitations on personal freedoms of speech, assembly, religion, and petition of grievances. It makes sense to compare nations as carefully as you consider brokers, bankers, bond ratings, or any other investment options.

For many, it makes sense to have some of their assets in another government jurisdiction to hedge against political trends in their own nation. That way, they can watch events at home unfold with the security of knowing that at least some of their property is outside the reach of their own government's greedy hands.

In 1928, U.S. Supreme Court Justice Louis Brandeis wrote, "They [the makers of the Constitution] conferred, as against the Government, the right to be let alone—the most comprehensive of rights and the right most valued by civilized men" (*Olmstead v. United States*, 277 U.S. 438, 478 [1928]). The irony of that frequently quoted statement is that Justice Brandeis was writing a *minority* opinion in the case, and his opinion has been in the minority among bureaucrats and politicians ever since. In the Olmstead case, the 5-to-4 majority gave the FBI permission to wiretap suspected gangsters, and such wiretapping is now widely considered a legitimate activity of government agencies. Let a little government in the door and you get a lot of government intervention down the line.

By 1971, with the passage of the grossly misnamed Bank

Secrecy Act in the United States, government access to private banking transactions became almost total. This law commands banks, among other things, to microfilm all checks of more than $100. The Bank Secrecy Act actually wipes out any pretense of privacy in banking transactions. The government has virtually deputized the banker to enforce federal policies instead of the customer's wishes.

In the United States, our financial lives have become totally transparent to the government. Notice how often you are asked for your Social Security number, even for nonfinancial applications. When you apply for any kind of loan or credit application, notice the breadth and depth of information that goes on your record—some of it having nothing to do with finances. On your Internal Revenue Service (IRS) 1040 form each April, notice the information being requested in detail. A complex return may include 10 or more pages of special schedules, listings of all companies paying you dividends, all banks paying you interest, etc. It seems the government doesn't just want our money; it wants to know every detail of our lives.

This financial information is kept in public and private files all over the nation. The IRS computer has every detail of your tax forms from over the years. The private credit files contain all the information you put on loan or insurance applications (e.g., health history). All your former employers have files on you. You would be amazed at the paper trail you have created by a lifetime of filling out forms.

Back in 1928, when Justice Brandeis eloquently expressed what the majority of Americans (if not justices) believed, there was a great heritage of privacy and independence in America. People did not share personal or financial information with their neighbors or even their children. "Silent Cal" Coolidge was president, and he exemplified the closed-mouth Yankee virtue of silence when he said, "I've never been hurt by anything I didn't say." And that says a lot.

Today, it is not uncommon to hear light cocktail banter about how much an investor has in T-bills, Swiss francs, bonds, and whatever else, or to brag about a "secret Swiss bank account" to a near-stranger, who just might be an undercover federal agent or an informer! We often hear people divulge their salary and outside income to anyone who asks or broadcast the value of their real estate, cars, or other possessions. The virtue of holding financial information in confidence has apparently been eroded badly since the days of Silent Cal.

In his novel *Cancer Ward*, Alexander Solzhenitsyn uses an interesting imagery about what government reporting looks (and feels) like: "As every man goes through life," he wrote, "he fills in a number of forms for the record, each containing a number of questions. There are thus hundreds of little threads radiating from every man, millions of threads in all, and if these threads were to suddenly become visible, the whole sky would look like a spider's web. They are not visible, they are not material, but every man is constantly aware of their existence."

It is possible to begin cutting away some of those threads or, at the very least, to limit the number of new informational threads being attached to us. We can first of all begin giving out less information about ourselves. It's possible to conduct financial matters without using checking accounts, which are microfilmed, or credit cards. You can use cashier's checks, traveler's checks, money orders, or cash. There are many ways to keep your financial affairs more private.

Second, we can conduct at least a portion of our banking and investment activity in a land that respects our financial privacy. If you compare the practices of your U.S. bankers to the practices of offshore bankers, it will become obvious to you that foreign bankers respect your money and your privacy, while their U.S. counterparts usually do not. Investors who overlook the stocks of overseas companies may be missing two-thirds of their opportunities.

U.S. issues represent little more than one-third of the world's total market in stock issues. And growth moves around. It was in Japan; now it is in Taiwan, Singapore, South Korea; in the future it will be in Thailand, even Vietnam. And don't overlook Latin America.

Mutual funds offer an easy way for investors to get involved in the stocks of foreign companies. So-called international funds invest solely in foreign companies; global funds mix in U.S. stocks. And, increasingly, the funds are focusing on specific countries or regions, such as Southeast Asia.

Investors can also buy pieces of the foreign companies directly, through American Depository Receipts (ADRs), which are traded on U.S. stock exchanges. ADRs, which represent shares of a foreign stock, are issued by U.S. banks that take possession of the securities. The banks convert dividend payments into dollars for ADR holders and deduct foreign withholding taxes.

ADRs give international investors a little more guarantee because those foreign companies have to meet certain accounting standards. For example, German companies that made only limited disclosures have to provide more information when moving into the U.S. markets.

Some investors dismiss investments in overseas companies as risky, but many of them are more conservative than their U.S. counterparts. For example, Swiss drug stocks typically have a price-to-earnings ratio of less than half that of U.S. companies. (Dividing a share's price by the company's earnings per share is a basic way to compare stock prices.)

Think of brand names known worldwide for investment potential. Companies such as Coca-Cola, Boeing, Disney, Ford, Citicorp, and Philip Morris are so multinational that they are not dependent on the U.S. economy, which is one of the things an investor would like to achieve.

There are good foreign bonds, too; it just takes more research to invest in suitable bonds.

Global investors must be patient. People invest in real estate and hold it for 10 or 15 years without thinking anything of it, but in stocks they often expect instant results.

Today there is a large and violent dependent population whose members demand that politicians protect them from falling living standards. But governments cannot fulfill this expectation. They are more bankrupt than ever before and likely to become more so. The impact of information technology will result in tens of millions of low-skilled service workers being made redundant in the next few years. This will lead to a further shortfall in tax revenues and more demands on politicians to redistribute income from an empty pocket.

Having some of your assets offshore will also provide a degree of protection against creditors and lawsuits. While this is not as complete as setting up an irrevocable trust, it does provide you with some advantages. By the time a claimant receives the proper authority to access your assets, you could have the account moved to another jurisdiction. The claimant may give up on those assets rather than continue to chase them.

It has been hard enough to convince individuals to look outside the conventional investment media of stocks, bonds, and life insurance for financial safety, but the idea that it might also be necessary for them to look outside the borders of the United States for capital protection is more than most can comprehend.

The reluctance of Americans to consider investing abroad is a natural consequence of their heritage. The U.S. dollar has been the strongest currency in the world during most of this century. The United States had a long history of protecting the property of individual citizens. The revolutions and wars that laid waste to other nations and destroyed the savings and investments of their citizens barely touched U.S. shores.

Most important of all, for the first 150 years of U.S. history, the individual was able to keep the major part of whatever he earned, either from his business or investments, without fear that the state would confiscate his gains. In total freedom, he could move his capital in and out of the country without the permission of government. In other words, the American investor kept his investment in his own country because of both the opportunities and the safety.

Today, growing numbers of investors are convinced that the United States is no longer the land of safety or opportunity. A few of the more astute investors are shedding their resistance to the idea of having their wealth kept thousands of miles away, across oceans and borders. There is a growing flight of U.S. capital abroad. But still, up until now, only the most adventurous of U.S. investors has actually taken the time and effort to look into the opportunities abroad. The great majority remain ignorant of both the reasons for needing to take their capital out of the country and the market mechanisms by which they can do it.

There are many countries today that fight their own domestic economic problems by holding their citizens' wealth hostage. The battle by citizens to evade these restrictions is documented by occasional news stories of important people being caught in the act of "smuggling" their own money across borders.

But just as citizens export their wealth to avoid its confiscation, so governments work diligently to close the escape routes. Foreign exchange controls, currency controls, credit controls, and taxes on foreign holdings are devices created by politicians to either freeze wealth within their jurisdiction (so they can confiscate it when ready) or to discourage people from bothering to take it abroad. As the flight of capital continues, even in the face of these laws, the laws are tightened, the severity of the penalties for capital export are increased, and the propaganda machine of government is turned fully against the "rich" speculators who are escaping with assets that "should rightly belong to the nation."

Escaping the net of the government is not the only reason you might want to place funds outside the country. There are certainly other legitimate benefits from such actions.

For instance, there might be investment opportunities available abroad that aren't available in the United States. While U.S.

real estate may be overpriced because of intensive government subsidy and intervention, comparable real estate in other markets is often selling at bargain-basement rates. World stock markets do not move in tandem; when the U.S. market is languishing, others may be booming. While savings accounts in U.S. banks may be guaranteed losers as the dollar depreciates, savings accounts in selected currencies in other countries consistently maintain the currencies' purchasing power.

Whatever happens, you want to be prepared in advance, and capital preservation through international diversification is a superb hedge against any contingency. The knowledge that a portion of your wealth is waiting for you, where nobody but you can touch it, creates a sense of security and a freedom from fear. That's something you can't put a price tag on.

GET YOUR WEALTH OUT
BEFORE EXCHANGE CONTROLS

When exchange controls take effect in any country, there is no warning. Most people don't realize that the United States already has such legislation on the books, ready for implementation by the president through executive order at any time. The International Emergency Economic Powers Act (Title II of Public Law 95-223) is a little-known act passed in 1977 without fanfare during the week between Christmas and the New Year. It gives the president complete power to "prohibit any transactions in foreign exchange," including "the importing or exporting of currency and securities" (Section 203a), in order "to deal with any unusual and extraordinary threat, which has its source in whole or substantial part outside the United States" (Section 202a). This act thus could prohibit all exchanges of currency, even wire transfers to other countries.

It has already been used by every president since it was passed. Carter used it against Iran, Reagan against the Soviet Union, and Bush Sr. against Iraq. But it could easily be used against any and all countries.

The growth of American investors' interest in global and international mutual funds is popularizing foreign investments in ways that may invoke such controls. And these U.S.-based mutual funds are the very ones that are most vulnerable to controls because they hold the money for tens of thousands of individual investors. In the right circumstances, it would not even be that difficult to order these funds to be liquidated and repatriate foreign holdings—an edict that would be difficult or impossible to enforce against individual investors with direct foreign investments.

Another forgotten law on the books is the Interest Equalization Tax Act. There is no reason for it to have been forgotten, but most investors (and most Americans) seem to have conveniently short memories. It is only 20 years since gold was legal for Americans to own, and the same length of time since the Interest Equalization Tax was lowered to zero. And that is the key—it was lowered to a temporary zero rate, not abolished or repealed. First enacted in 1964, it put a 15-percent tax on all purchases of foreign securities. It could be raised again at any time, and this time it would also affect all purchases by U.S. mutual funds investing internationally. Such funds did not exist in 1964, but they do now—and are very vulnerable. Such a tax would not affect their existing holdings, but what happens to a fund that could only hold its existing securities and not replace them with other foreign securities? The whole management aspect of the fund is destroyed, and management is what you are paying a mutual fund to do for you. The inability to manage would likely cause a run on all these funds, with forced liquidations to meet redemptions causing distress sales of portfolio holdings—or a suspension of redemptions.

INVEST WISELY

One of the often neglected areas of the investment of an American's money in an offshore environment is what the actual investment scenario may be. Many times Americans enter a world with which they are unfamiliar and do not recognize the significant risks there can be in investing in a world where issues of bonds, stocks, annuities, CDs, and the like are done in an unpredictable and unknown environment.

It is imperative that domestic investors be aware of the risks that they are taking and the market conditions they are entering. More times than not, what the less than professional investor should do is seek professional and accredited money management. If one were to turn to world-class organizations (and avoid a lot of the current offshore hype that saturates the Internet in particular), many times the unwieldy and unknown aspects of international investment would become easy and routine to deal with.

A decade or two ago, offshore havens were used primarily by wealthy families setting up trusts for the grandchildren. As tax laws have changed, such simple solutions are generally no longer possible.

But today the same countries are being used, with the same trust and corporate forms, to provide asset protection. The tax neutrality of the tax haven countries is ideal for this purpose, since there is no additional tax complication for the person seeking asset protection. Thus the tax-haven business has slowly evolved into the asset-protection business.

It is preferable by far to stay with jurisdictions where the asset protection features have evolved as a fundamental part of the law and the local social and political structure. The Swiss law protecting insurance policies from seizure has been in effect since 1908—not to attract foreign business but because the Swiss wanted it to protect themselves. A Swiss court isn't going to look for excuses to carve exceptions out of the law.

Panama has been a corporate management center since it became a country because that business was an integral part of the commercial center that developed around the Panama Canal.

The Isle of Man has long served British expatriates who work around the world, and the banking, trust, and company management expertise developed there is well educated and conservative.

HOW TO BEST USE THIS BOOK

Using offshore havens is an art not a science, which means that you will find contradictions in this book. One of the things to bear in mind when studying an art is that taste plays a role. The offshore strategy that suits the needs, and prejudices, of one person may not suit those of another. It is not an exact science that can be replicated through experiments and demonstrations.

Most of these decisions are somewhat subjective, and depend on your personality and your personal experience as much as they do on law. You have to go with the people, countries, and cultures you feel comfortable with.

People frequently ask what the best offshore haven is or what the best country in which to open a bank account is. There is no "best" answer—these things are very personal and depend on what you want to do.

The cultural issues are a two-way street. Americans are used to sending off a postcard to ask for literature on an investment. Most foreign firms, and European ones in particular, don't do business that way. In many cases they've been around a few centuries, and they don't need your business. They are far more concerned with whether or not you are suitable person for them to even be talking about, and a "please send all your information" request from an American is likely to go into the wastebasket unanswered. Take the time to write a proper letter, in proper format, introducing yourself, explaining why you are interested in the firm, and telling enough to establish that you are a responsible and respectable person who is suited to having an account with the firm. These firms want to know whom they are dealing with just as much as you want to, so requesting information using a false name at a mail drop is not the way to establish the appropriate relationship.

Over the years a number of firms have asked that I not mention them in my publications, primarily because they don't care for difficult relationships with Americans. One private banker mentioned that Americans tend to open an account, then boast about it at cocktail parties, and eventually the wife's divorce lawyers show up with a claim for half the account and want to drag the bank into litigation. A Swiss banker, discussing his bank's requirements stated: "$1 million if it is an Argentinian, $10 million if it is an American—they're more trouble than they're worth." In the past five years, many European banks and stockbrokers have simply closed all accounts belonging to U.S. citizens rather than deal with both the customers' personalities and the U.S. government's increasing demands for information.

With proper effort you can have a wonderful relationship with some of the best banks and financial services in the world, but please take a moment to think about how you appear to them before you engage in any communication.

Chapter 1

How to Make Really Big Money Investing Globally

ne of the most valuable elements of offshore investing is the ability to compound earnings tax free. This factor alone is a major reason for selecting offshore opportunities over domestic investments.

THE VALUE OF TAX-FREE COMPOUND INTEREST

Much of the discussion of the growing value of an investment depends on the tax-free compounding of the earnings.

Everyone knows about the "miracle of compound interest"—stories of what a dollar left in the bank by your grandfather would be worth 100 years later at 6 percent per year, or a penny left by Columbus. It is such a cliché that almost everyone ignores the powerful, fundamental truth underlying the concept. And few people understand how to make compound interest work for them.

Compounding is a two-way street. Debts get compounded, too. That is why so many "wealthy" people are going bankrupt, for example. Back in the 1970s and 1980s, the fashion of the time was to buy U.S. real estate leveraged with debt and roll over the debt, counting on an increase in the value of the property to pay off the debt and make a profit. And in much of the United States, real estate values did increase at a rate that enabled a lot of people to make a lot of money purely on debt financing. They would pay for a property with borrowed money, sometimes 90 percent or more of the total value. (The banks played along with this game. They made money too as long as prices were rising.)

Instead of paying off the loan, they would allow the principal and interest to build. At 10-percent interest, after a year the principal on a $100,000 loan would grow to $110,000. In five years it would be a monstrous $161,000, and so on.

The trouble is, real estate values don't go in one direction only. They also go down, as they are now doing in many parts of the world. All that built-up, compounded debt eventually has to be paid, and very often real estate investors do not have the means to actually pay off the debt they contracted. They never expected to have to do so.

The secret of compound interest is to be on the right side of it. Debts compound, and so do costs. Being on the right side of compounding means positioning investments so that time works for them rather than against them. When investments are positioned properly, each passing day adds to their value, free from taxes and inflation.

More than 2,000 years ago the Greek philosopher Aristotle explained that the secret to success in anything was *habit* (Aristotle used the word *ethos*). To him it was the crucial ingredient of all genius. Habit is nothing more than a recognition of the concept of compound interest applied to life itself.

Aristotle recognized that people do not simply wake up one day with the idea for a great invention . . . or jump to the command of a great army . . . or write down a marvelous essay . . . or get rich.

All progress is made by small increments compounding over time. A great thinker thinks hard for a long time and, over time, comes up with great thoughts. A great builder lays one brick at a time and, over time, builds great monuments. A great artist works day after day and, over time, produces great works of art. So too, a man builds his wealth a little each day and, over time, becomes very rich.

The idea of building wealth over time has a kind of tedious ring to it, but you cannot ignore the power of compounding. With compounding, time adds to value. Instead of being tedious, the passage of time in the investment plan becomes an important ingredient that turns the capital into more.

Thus the "miracle of compound interest." It is based on a powerful, fundamental truth, although too few people understand how to make compound interest work for them. The results are incredible. A 20-percent annual return on your investment free of tax compounds to a sum 1,200 percent more over a lifetime than the same sum with tax. It is the difference between $8 million and $100 million over 40 years. And the same magic applies when you start with smaller amounts.

I do want to stress that just because money is offshore does not automatically mean it is tax free. It is important that a proper and legal structure be used to keep the money tax free, either through annuities, trusts, or other structures that you choose only after proper accounting and legal advice.

Putting $2,000 a year into a tax-free account investing in stocks that pay 10 percent dividends means $35,062.31 after 10 years—not including any capital gains. Table 1 shows how this works. Start with a $2,000 contribution and add $2,000 tax free each year. For example, if you are contributing to an individual retirement account (IRA) account, which has a $2,000 annual limit, after 25 years, you'd have $216,363.29. On the other hand, an annuity has no maximum limit, so you can contribute more.

TABLE 1: TAX-FREE SAVINGS (INCLUDING DIVIDENDS)

Years	Beginning	End
1	$2,000.00	$2,200.00
2	$4,200.00	$4,620.00
3	$6,620.00	$7,282.00
4	$9,282.00	$10,210.20
5	$12,210.20	$13,431.22
6	$15,431.22	$16,974.34
7	$18,974.34	$20,871.77
8	$22,871.77	$25,158.94
9	$27,158.94	$29,874.83
10	$31,874.83	$35,062.31
11	$37,062.31	$40,768.54
12	$42,768.54	$47,045.39
13	$49,045.39	$53,949.92
14	$55,949.92	$61,544.91
15	$63,544.91	$69,899.40
16	$71,899.40	$79,089.34
17	$81,089.34	$89,198.27
18	$91,198.27	$100,318.09
19	$102,318.09	$112,549.89
20	$114,549.89	$126,004.87
21	$128,004.87	$140,805.35
22	$142,805.35	$157,085.88
23	$159,085.88	$174,994.46
24	$176,994.46	$194,693.90
25	$196,693.90	$216,363.29

Compounding this kind of income from investments is a guaranteed way to build wealth, without any extra risks or effort. Once the wealth-building strategy is in place, it's just a matter of time. Most investors are looking for extraordinary capital gains—and most fail to realize how hard it is to achieve that. Wealth-building investors should seek investments offering decent dividends or interest and let that yield compound. To think of it another way, look at Table 2:

TABLE 2: AMOUNTS AT COMPOUND INTEREST
(Multiply the Principal by the Factor in the Table)

Years	1%	2%	3%	4%	5%	6%	7%
1	1.0100	1.0200	1.0300	1.0400	1.0500	1.0600	1.0700
2	1.0201	1.0404	1.0609	1.0816	1.1025	1.1236	1.1449
3	1.0303	1.0612	1.0927	1.1249	1.1576	1.1910	1.2250
4	1.0406	1.0824	1.1255	1.1699	1.2155	1.2625	1.3108
5	1.0510	1.1041	1.1593	1.2167	1.2763	1.3382	1.4026
6	1.0615	1.1262	1.1941	1.2653	1.3401	1.4185	1.5007
7	1.0721	1.1487	1.2299	1.3159	1.4071	1.5036	1.6058
8	1.0829	1.1717	1.2668	1.3686	1.4775	1.5938	1.7182
9	1.0937	1.1951	1.3048	1.4233	1.5513	1.6895	1.8385
10	1.1046	1.2190	1.3439	1.4802	1.6289	1.7908	1.9672
11	1.1157	1 2434	1.3842	1.5395	1.7103	1.8983	2.1049
12	1.1268	1 2682	1.4258	1.6010	1.7959	2.0122	2.2522
13	1.1381	1.2936	1.4685	1.6651	1.8856	2.1329	2.4098
14	1.1495	1.3195	1.5126	1.7317	1.9799	2.2609	2.5785
15	1.1610	1.3459	1.5580	1.8009	2.0789	2.3966	2.7590
16	1.1726	1.3728	1.6047	1.8730	2.1829	2.5404	2.9522
17	1.1843	1.4002	1.6528	1.9479	2.2920	2.6928	3.1588
19	1.2081	1.4568	1.7535	2.1068	2.5270	3.0256	3.6165
20	1.2202	1.4859	1.8061	2.1911	2.6533	3.2071	3.8697
21	1.2324	1.5157	1.8603	2.2788	2.7860	3.3996	4.1406
22	1.2447	1.5460	1.9161	2.3699	2.9253	3.6035	4.4304
23	1.2572	1.5769	1.9736	2.4647	3.0715	3.8197	4.7405
24	1.2697	1.6084	2.0328	2.5633	3.2251	4.0489	5.0724
25	1.2824	1.6406	2.0938	2.6658	3.3864	4.2919	5.4274
26	1.2953	1.6734	2.1566	2.7725	3.5557	4.5494	5.8074
27	1.3082	1.7069	2.2213	2.8834	3.7335	4.8223	6.2139
28	1.3213	1.7410	2.2213	2.9987	3.9201	5.1117	6.6488
29	1.3345	1.7758	2.3566	3.1187	4.1161	5.4184	7.1143
30	1.3476	1.8114	2.4773	3.7434	4.3219	5.7435	7.6123

TABLE 2: AMOUNTS AT COMPOUND INTEREST (cont'd.)
(Multiply the Principal by the Factor in the Table)

Years	8%	9%	10%	11%	12%	13%
1	1.0800	1.0900	1.1000	1.1100	1.1200	1.1300
2	1.1664	1.1881	1.2100	1.2321	1.2544	1.2769
3	1.2597	1.2950	1.3310	1.3676	1.4049	1.4429
4	1.3605	1.4116	1.4641	1.5181	1.5735	1.6305
5	1.4693	1.5386	1.6105	1.6851	1.7623	1.8424
6	1.5869	1.6771	1.7716	1.8704	1.9738	2.0820
7	1.7138	1.8280	1.9487	2.0762	2.2107	2.3526
8	1.8509	1.9926	2.1436	2.3045	2.4760	2.6584
9	1.9990	2.1719	2.3579	2.5580	2.7731	3.0040
10	2.1589	2.3674	2.5937	2.8394	3.1058	3.3946
11	2.3316	2.5804	2.8531	3.1518	3.4785	3.8359
12	2.5182	2.8127	3.1384	3.4985	3.8960	4.3345
13	2.7196	3.0658	3.4523	3.8833	4.3635	4.8980
14	2.9372	3.3417	3.7975	4.3104	4.8871	5.5348
15	3.1722	3.6425	4.1772	4.7846	5.4736	6.2543
16	3.4259	3.9703	4.5950	5.3109	6.1304	7.0673
17	3.7000	4.3276	5.0545	5.8951	6.8660	7.9861
18	3.9960	4.7171	5.5599	6.5436	7.6900	9.0243
19	4.3157	5.1417	6.1159	7.2633	8.6128	10.0197
20	4.6610	5.6044	6.7275	8.0623	9.6463	11.5231
21	5.0338	6.1088	7.4002	8.9492	10.8038	13.0211
22	5.4365	6.6586	8.1403	9.9336	12.1003	14.7138
23	5.8715	7.2579	8.9543	11.0263	13.5523	16.6266
24	6.3412	7.9111	9.8497	12.2392	15.1786	18.7881
25	6.8485	8.6231	10.8347	13.5855	17.0001	21.2305
26	7.3964	9.3992	11.9182	15.0797	19.0401	23.9905
27	7.9881	10.2451	13.1100	16.7386	21.3249	27.1093
28	8.6271	11.1671	14.4210	18.5799	23.8839	30.6335
29	9.3173	12.1722	15.8631	20.6237	26.7499	34.6158
30	10.0627	13.2677	17.4494	22.8923	29.9599	39.1159

Chapter 2

Of Morality and Patriotism

Should you support the government's efforts to keep your money inside its borders because it is patriotic, good for the nation, ethical, or moral?

First, it is imperative that we establish exactly the purposes of international diversification of your assets and the political implications. This book examines a highly effective method of asset protection and growth. But who really wants to protect his assets and reduce his taxes? The question may seem naive, even stupid. After all, who doesn't want to keep more of what's his? But this sort of answer, derived from the cynical "everyone is selfish" notion, is not what we are looking for.

Self-sufficiency and wealth protection through the use of international financial strategies and diversification require considerable initiative, alertness, determination, and dedication. Not that it doesn't pay. Sad to say, the net gain from each hour dedicated to protecting your wealth is almost certain to be higher than the net gain from an hour of productive employment. Thanks to "progressive" taxation, this goes double for someone in a relatively high tax bracket. There is also a psychological dimension that must not be neglected. Most people derive a "clean" feeling from making a living through their work but feel that there is something dirty about scheming to reduce their taxes.

Heavy taxes, whether used to provide luxury for a ruling elite or to support welfare schemes, always penalize individual initiative and productivity; restrict investment capital and thus the resources required for economic growth; reduce the standard of living; and force individuals to hide things, both activities and incomes, from the government and from one another. Heavy taxation is, therefore, a danger to the future of the high-tax countries.

Internationalizing assets assumes at the outset that the investor has assets available for investment. It also assumes that a viable means of doing so exists in the contemporary scheme of world business and, ideally, that a plan exists that includes short- and long-range investment goals.

To consider the question of the morality of diversification and tax avoidance, it is first necessary to set forth a working definition of the word *morality*. In this context, morality is not considered an absolute, but a concept that, like the laws themselves, is subject to interpretation. One person might argue quite convincingly that it is morally wrong to tax a working widow with children to help provide support for a war veteran who is able to work but prefers not to; another person can argue just as convincingly on behalf of the veteran. Others would argue the libertarian position that all taxation is theft.

The morality of taxation changes with the times. Prior to World War I, when taxes were comparatively low, though certainly not popular, most workers and small businessmen were exempt from the controversy by virtue of low incomes. During times of national emergency, particularly during and directly following World War II, tax avoidance was frowned upon even by those who were looking at larger tax liabilities each year. But as progressive rates took taxes higher and higher each year in highly industrialized and populated nations, the attitudes of taxpayers underwent a gradual but definitive change.

Today, even the individual worker for whom the tax system is supposedly designed can see that a tax system in which higher income brackets produce progressively higher tax rates is stultifying to individual initiative and productivity. Investors feel not only duty bound but morally obligated to use the legal tax avoidance measures available to them. Whether the tax loss to the nation is through the use of domestic tax shelter strategies or an international financial center, the avoidance principle is exactly the same. From a purely pragmatic viewpoint, legal tax avoidance by an investor may not be the road to wealth but simply a means of economic survival for himself and his family.

The losers in this business of tax avoidance are presumed to be the heavily industrialized, heavily populated, and heavily taxed countries of the world. If two nations could personify this description, they would be the United States and Great Britain. Yet the attitudes of these governments toward tax avoidance is ambivalent, to say the least. The United States, for example, actually established itself as a tax haven for foreigners by not imposing a withholding tax on interest paid to foreigners from their U.S. bank deposits and by allowing foreigners to buy, hold, and sell U.S. securities without incurring a capital gains liability.

There are, of course, economic reasons to justify these tax rulings (a reversal of the ruling on interest paid from bank deposits would remove billions of dollars from U.S. banks). This being the case, we can say that there is no external threat to tax avoidance from free world nations. The United States and Switzerland are both involved in the business of providing a haven for foreign investors to protect their assets. The citizens of each frequently use the other for international diversification, and neither is likely to try to put the other out of business.

It was bad enough when it was only a national issue, but the past few years have seen increasing moves from international bodies—including the United Nations, the Organization for Economic Cooperation and Development, the European Union (EU), and others—to "harmonize" national tax policies, preventing tax haven countries from competing to offer lower taxes than the industrialized nations. It used to be acceptable that economies competed—so this new attitude is a dangerous trend. Never before have offshore havens been the target of such virulent attacks as those in 2000 and 2001. International organizations have charged that tax havens (1) rob prosperous industrialized countries of their tax revenues; (2) permit too much bank, corporate, and individual secrecy; and 3) lack vigor in the fight against money laundering.

At the time of this writing it is difficult to know where it will all come out, but the speed of these international actions has been much faster than the usual glacial pace of international treaties and regulations, and you need to watch out for these changes in the laws and the political climate in the years ahead.

International enforcement of tax obligations has begun with some agreement between the United States and Great Britain, and it is likely that other countries will soon join this pattern. The EU continues to make threatening noises about harmonization and enforcement among all European countries. Clearly, we have reached the end of the accepted international position that tax laws and their enforcement were purely domestic and could not be enforced in the courts of other nations.

The arguments that apply to taxation apply even more strongly to asset preservation through international diversification. Much of the growth in China today is being funded by Chinese investors in Hong Kong who got their capital out of China during the communist takeover and are now providing the funds to restore capitalism to their country.

Preservation of wealth often involves a timely decision to move capital from one place, or one form, to another. Many times, capital would have been lost if it had not been wisely redeployed as circumstances changed. Capital is always under political threat when it is in a minority. The periods of greatest risk are times of public disorder when many are impoverished and only a few are wise enough or lucky enough to preserve their wealth.

In 1931 Britain went off the gold standard. At that time investments in gold coins could be bought for £100, which would now sell for £50,000, while government bonds could be bought for £100 and would now sell for £30. Yet in 1931, government bonds were thought a safer investment than gold coins and were the only investments allowed for most trustees.

This shows how families can rapidly be reduced from prosperity to poverty. The difference between two investments in one lifetime could easily amount to one investment rising 12 times as fast as inflation while the other falls to roughly 1 percent of its original purchasing power. Take the experience of what happened in one generation in Britain as a likely model for what could easily lie ahead for North America.

Government destroys capital. Allowing it to destroy yours is not a rational path to prosperity or security. To whatever extent the government is successful, production falls. The more you feed the crocodile, the bigger it grows.

The one clear answer is self-protection. But how? This book will show that there are ways—very elegant solutions that are completely legal and risk free.

Chapter 3

Forfeitures and Lawsuits

*I*n the past, it was the practice in this country that when a person wished to retain a lawyer to sue someone he would pay the lawyer a fee, and the lawyer would examine the issues and then proceed based on the merits of the case. This is no longer the case.

The contingency system now in place means that we have lawsuits filed at the rate of one hundred million each year. Many of these suits have nothing to do with right and wrong, but, instead, are predicated on the desire of one party to extract wealth from another party. In many cases, this equation is based not on the desire to extract real wealth, but rather on a desire to extract small payments as "nuisance" settlements because it is often cheaper for the defendant to pay the money than to fight the suit.

If this was not bad enough, it is also a problem for those who are not sued, because another part of the problem is in the cost to the taxpayers of maintaining the court system to handle this litigation.

If we assume that one is lucky enough to make it through the legal maze without becoming a target, then at time of death the federal government under today's law would take roughly 50 percent of a family's wealth as the transfer is made from mother and father to children of all amounts over $1.2 million. Several bills have been proposed that would enact even more onerous taxation.

If you have attempted to pursue the American dream of wealth, independence, and self-determination, you may very well be disappointed by these facts. In fact, you may be frightened. You may, for the first time in your life, even be considering leaving the country. According to *Money* magazine, at least 250,000 people per year move out of the United States. Most of these people move for better business opportunities, a better environment to raise their children, or other reasons that have nothing to do with lawsuits (or taxes). But foreign residence is a step that should be seriously considered.

For many people the threshold issue in moving assets offshore for protection is "do I need it?" Many people believe that "this won't happen to me," "it can't happen to my business," or "my family is safe because we don't do anything that's dangerous. " The reality of life in the United States is that you don't have to do anything dangerous; all you really have to do is be in the wrong place at the wrong time. Ordinary people have extraordinary problems. In many cases these problems are not problems of their own doing; they are simply matters of circumstance.

Imagine a group of business partners getting together for an informal lunch to discuss their work. One member of the secretarial staff is asked to go to a local restaurant and pick up a food order for these partners. Unbeknown to them, this secretary has a poor driving record, which includes several accidents and speeding tickets. The secretary leaves the building, climbs into a company car, and picks up the lunch order. On her way back to the office, driving faster than the posted speed and paying more attention to the radio than the upcoming stop sign, she fails to stop and smashes into another car, taking the life of its driver. A subsequent lawsuit, one should think, would simply blame the employee for her negligence; but this is not the case.

All the business partners are sued as the result of their negligence in not determining that this driver was in fact unsafe. More important, this driver was on company business, and the heirs of the accident victim now seek retribution from those partners. The partners' homes, children's college funds, boats, vacation homes, and even business are up for grabs.

In many such cases one of the prime financial elements being sought is insurance. In days gone by, insurance was a protector of the family and the business, but nowadays it often becomes a target.

CIVIL ASSET FORFEITURE: THE RISK
PEOPLE DON'T WANT TO TALK ABOUT

Forfeiture is even more difficult to protect against than lawsuits. For this reason, many people feel that domestic lawsuit protection strategies are inadequate, because as long as the assets are located in the United States, they can be forfeited, regardless of trusts, partnerships, or other ways of titling the assets that may protect them from ordinary lawsuits.

Any property-owning U.S. citizen, and any investor with property in the United States, must become knowledgeable about the threat of civil asset forfeiture—the government's police power to confiscate your real and personal property, based on that property's alleged use or involvement in criminal activities.

The threat of government confiscation applies to homeowners; landlords; people with a resort condominium; investors or partners in hotels, restaurants, and bars; and those who own undeveloped or farmland. Even retail business and commercial property owners are at serious risk.

For people concerned about protecting their wealth, particularly real estate, avoidance of potential asset forfeiture is a compelling reason to take careful preventive action—or to avoid certain types of real estate investments completely. Avoidance of civil asset forfeiture is not an easy task, especially because of investor complacency based on a traditional belief in a host of U.S. constitutional safeguards for private property ownership. Alarmingly, many of these former legal protections have collapsed under the pressure of a growing U.S. police state.

Civil asset forfeiture laws are being enforced with Gestapo-like zeal by state and federal police authorities and courts in a highly unjust manner. These questionable official acts, literally robbing private citizens, depend for their dubious authority on a combination of musty legal doctrines dating back to early English common law and the eagerness of contemporary politicians to "get tough" on crime and drugs, even at the expense of personal liberty.

A standard legal dictionary definition of *forfeiture,* until a few years ago, was the "loss of some right or property as a penalty for some illegal act." Whether you call it forfeiture, confiscation, expropriation, or commandeering, it all amounts to the same thing: government now has the arbitrary power to seize almost any privately owned property. Property is in danger of seizure if it is (1) *allegedly* purchased with the proceeds of illegal activity; (2) *allegedly* used to "facilitate" criminal activity, or (3) *allegedly* the location of criminal activity.

The word *allegedly* is emphasized because the statutory and judicial procedures governing forfeitures allow police to seize your property—prior to any hearing before a judge or magistrate—and to keep the property without charging you with any crime. The government has the right to retain it until you are able to prove your property is not tainted by criminal conduct.

Much of what you may have learned in the past about your guaranteed rights and liberties no longer applies to property rights. Increased government and police powers, the perception of rising criminal activity and violence, popular anxiety about drug use—all these were the political justifications for curtailing the application of the Bill of Rights and the individual security it once guaranteed. Police and government agents now have the power to seize your business, home, bank account, records, and personal property, all without prior indictment, hearing, or trial. Everything you possess can be taken away at the whim of one or two state or federal officials who may target you secretly. Regardless of sex, age, race, or economic status, we are all just a knock on the door away from becoming potential victims of civil asset forfeiture and its abuse.

Lest you mistakenly believe the notion that asset forfeiture only concerns drug-related crimes, you should know there are now more than 100 different federal forfeiture statutes, addressing a wide range of illegal conduct, both criminal and civil.

Some of the federal government agencies with statutory forfeiture power include the Drug Enforcement Administration and the U.S. Customs Bureau of the Treasury Department, the Federal Bureau of Investigation, the U.S. Coast Guard, the U.S. Postal Service, the Bureau of Land Management and the Fish and Wildlife Bureau (both in the Interior Department), the Securities and Exchange Commission, the Department of Health and Human Services, the Food and Drug Administration, the Justice Department (including the Immigration and Naturalization Service), the Department of Housing and Urban Development, and, of course, the Internal Revenue Service—plus more than 3,000 state and local police departments.

New Jersey is a state with one of the most severe forfeiture laws, triggered by any alleged criminal conduct, even shoplifting. The theory is that you took the stolen property home, so the authorities can seize the car you took it home in, the house you stored it in, and so forth. That statute denies the right to a trial by jury on the issue of forfeiture. Its application is so severe that a male gynecologist, Owen A. Chang, M.D., accused of conducting a medical exam of a female patient without the presence of a nurse, as required by local law, had his office equipment and building confiscated. Kathy Schrama, accused of stealing packages delivered by UPS worth at most $500 from her neighbors' doorsteps in New Jersey, saw local police take away her home, two cars, and all her furniture—even the Christmas presents she had purchased for her 10-year-old son. A building contractor who bid on, received, properly executed, and was paid for several construction contracts for New Jersey municipalities later had his entire business confiscated by the state based on an allegation that his company was not legally qualified to make the bids in the first place.

Arizona's statutes also provide an example of the trend in abandoning any distinction between civil and criminal forfeiture, applying unlimited forfeiture with few procedural protections for property owners as a handy supplement to criminal law enforcement. The state's assistant attorney general, Cameron Holmes, proudly describes his state's law as "a stride in the evolution of a 'civil justice system' to complement the 'criminal justice system' through judicial intervention in antisocial behavior." This is the sort of exceedingly fuzzy thinking that has served to expand property confiscation and shrink personal legal protection and freedom.

Not content with applying forfeiture law to drug offenses, legislators and prosecutors are rapidly expanding the forfeiture principle to cover a host of alleged criminal acts in every area of activity. A growing number of states, including Texas, New Jersey, and Florida, now apply civil forfeiture to any criminal activity, which means owners must police their real property against all criminal activity or possibly lose it. Homeowners and landlords are not only being forced into the role of "their brother's keeper," but are being held responsible for the acts of their children, spouse, guests, and tenants—and even their tenant's guests.

The New York City Police Department learned a valuable

lesson from state and national law enforcement agencies, and in 2000 began its "Zero Tolerance Drinking and Driving Initiative." The stated goal of this program is to discourage drunk driving and means that anyone arrested for drunk driving in New York City will have his car seized until he is acquitted of the charges. The policy is based on the fact that city code permits police to seize "instrumentalities of crime."

Make a mistake on a loan application and you may face forfeiture. In an attempt to curb savings and loan fraud, in 1989 Congress made it a criminal offense to give false information on a loan application. Now this law is being used by the government to confiscate the property financed with loan proceeds, even years later, and even if all payments are up to date. Under this loan application law, in Florida in 1991, the U.S. Marshal's Service seized $11 million worth of commercial property, including five convenience stores, a multiplex movie theater, and a consumer electronics store.

To give you an idea of how far this has gone, in 1993 a federal circuit court ruled that defendants charged with illegally modifying, selling, and using television signal "descramblers" (which allow satellite dishes to pick up coded TV signals) were violating federal wiretapping laws. Such acts are not only felonies but forfeiture crimes, meaning that your house could be taken away if you install a TV signal descrambler.

The state of Missouri, to keep police forces from temptation, designated the proceeds from forfeitures to its public schools. However, greed being an inherent part of human nature, the police agencies have found a way to circumvent state law and keep seized property for their own use. When the police uncover, for example, money from a drug deal, they then turn it over to a federal agency, which keeps a percentage and returns the rest to the police. In fact, a federal judge from the 8th U.S. Circuit Court of Appeals found that the federal Drug Enforcement Administration and the Missouri Highway Patrol had conspired to keep forfeited cash.

These forfeiture laws are little known, and although these

examples show how widely they are used, most people tend to brush off the news and think, "Well, those guys must have done something illegal." None of this information is that hard to find—much of it is published in required legal notices of the forfeitures in daily newspapers, but people just don't pay attention to its significance—until it is too late and it is their property being seized. *Time* and *Newsweek* have covered these stories frequently—and were the source of many of the incidents listed here. You had a chance to read them too. Did you? And did you think about it? (Although a number of cases have been given as examples, the final outcomes may vary through litigation, which often takes years, so the final results may not be the same as given at the time of writing.)

As you begin to see, the possibilities of you and your property being ensnared by government forfeiture are endless.

Chapter 4

Fools Spend
Time in Prison

ne of the greatest problems of offshore priva-
cy strategic planning is the fool who breaks
laws without thinking through the consequences. For example, as a consultant, I once
had a call from a certified public accountant in
a major U.S. city who said he had a number of
clients who wanted to establish "secret" bank
accounts in the Cayman Islands. He said his
clients were paying all their taxes but were
very concerned with secrecy and wanted to be
certain that the U.S. government would not
learn about the accounts.

He became greatly offended when I
explained to him that all his clients were
crooks. I explained in detail that no U.S. citizen
(or resident) could have a "secret" bank
account because it is a felony to fail to notify
the government immediately of the existence
of the account. The penalties for such secrecy at
that time were far worse than any possible tax
offense—today the penalties have been

increased so much that no American should even contemplate such a violation. One bribed bank clerk (perhaps for a mere $100) in a so-called secrecy jurisdiction could put the client in prison for 10 to 15 years under new mandatory minimum sentencing laws. There are numerous legitimate ways that a U.S. citizen can make foreign investments without running afoul of these draconian laws, which will be discussed later in this book.

The most dangerous fools—to themselves as well as to everyone they deal with—are those who fail to understand the seriousness of the implications of their actions. These fools deal with lawyers, accountants, or bankers as if there was nothing legally wrong with their actions and then seem startled when the family accountant or banker facing many years in prison testifies against them because he was dragged into something he had no intention of being a part of. Or, worse, they wind up blurting out their self-incriminating intentions to a lawyer or accountant who immediately notifies the authorities, frequently setting a trap for them. (Remember, lawyer-client confidentiality does not apply to stating an intention to commit a crime, and the lawyer is legally obligated to report it.) Many U.S. professionals today (perhaps fearing a possible setup by authorities) err on the side of caution and immediately report such approaches. This is no secret—it has been recorded in many, many court cases—but naive clients continue to get convicted. One of the recent trends has been for other countries to pass similar laws, usually under pressure from international bodies to fight "money laundering."

The penalties for most of the bank secrecy and money-laundering crimes (money laundering includes moving unreported cash, even if you are the legal owner) are several times the penalty for armed bank robbery.

Most of these people would never consider committing a bank robbery, and if they were to plan such a crime, they would choose their partners with extreme care and full awareness of the consequences to all parties concerned. Yet they think nothing of committing financial crimes with far more serious penalties and cavalierly involving others, as if it was a big joke and nothing to be seriously concerned about.

There are enough legal means to accomplish the same ends that nobody needs to commit these crimes. But if individuals persist in doing so, they should at least face the reality of their acts and plan like real criminals, choosing their associates with the same care they would use to choose bank robbery partners. If you really want to be a criminal, then be one, but don't stagger around the offshore banking world like a drunken water buffalo.

If you want to gain a good understanding of how the government views tax havens, read *Tax Havens and Their Uses by United States Taxpayers* by Richard Gordon, which was prepared by the U.S. Treasury Department at the request of Congress. Frequently referred to as "The Gordon Report," this 1981 study gives considerable detail and examples of the uses of tax havens. Anyone interested in tax havens who has not studied this work will find much of its information still useful and gain familiarity with the flavor of government thinking in the field. Although out of print for several years, it has been reissued by a commercial publisher, and copies can be ordered through booksellers.

Chapter 5

Offshore
Bank Accounts

 key to taking advantage of offshore secrecy havens is the offshore bank account. It can be used as part of an aggressive wealth-building strategy or a defensive wealth-preservation and asset-protection plan. It was not many years ago that a person needed to be wealthy to benefit from an offshore bank account. But international banking and communications have changed dramatically. The offshore bank account is now a quick, inexpensive entry to foreign investment opportunities and other benefits.

Such bank accounts inspire many images in people's minds. There are visions of international drug dealers laundering billions of dollars in drug profits through Panamanian, Bahamian, and other offshore banks. Others think of the CIA setting up front organizations for its operations and using offshore accounts to pay for expenses, informants, and operatives. Offshore bank accounts have been used to conceal bribes paid to foreign officials, even royalty. The Iran-Contra operation allegedly involved the extensive use of foreign bank accounts.

Although these images and stories make for good reading, they have little to do with our present purposes, which are to make money and to protect our assets. The offshore bank account is a highly effective and economic way to achieve those goals.

USES OF THE OFFSHORE BANK ACCOUNT

The offshore bank account allows you to invest in foreign stocks and mutual funds that are not registered with U.S. government agencies. The account also might carry transaction costs lower than those of other methods.

An offshore bank account offers more options than most U.S. accounts. You can use the account as a way to profit from currency fluctuations, buy stocks or mutual funds, purchase foreign real estate, and earn the high interest rates available in many foreign countries. You also can trade precious metals and other assets through most foreign accounts.

The offshore bank account provides a measure of asset protection. The existence of the offshore account will not readily be known by someone seeking to collect against your assets. The account probably will be revealed in your tax returns, and you will be legally obliged to include it in any required statement of your assets. But the creditor will have to file a separate court action and get a separate judgment in the country in which the account is located. This allows you time to fight the action or simply move the assets out of the account, unless the court immediately issues an order prohibiting you from transferring any assets, which ordinarily does not happen.

You can achieve a great measure of safety in an offshore bank account. You might have noticed that the banking crises of the 1980s and 1990s were largely not international ones. Primarily, it was U.S. banks and savings and loans that were failing. Many foreign banks had established U.S. branches and invested in U.S. real estate. Yet these banks were not failing. That is because they operate under different rules and have more reasonable financial practices than even the strongest U.S. banks. In many developed countries, on the rare occasion when a bank fails the major banks in the country take over its business to ensure that depositors do not lose any money. So if you are looking for banking safety, you should consider offshore banks.

An offshore bank can offer a measure of privacy not available in the United States. Many foreign countries ensure banking privacy in all but the most extreme situations. Even Switzerland, which recently changed its rules about numbered accounts. In the past, the fabled numbered Swiss account would be opened with only one bank officer knowing the true identity of the account owner. Those days are gone, and bank records now must record the identity of each account's owner. In spite of this change, numbered accounts still are available and provide a great deal of privacy.

OPENING THE OFFSHORE ACCOUNT

It is fairly simple to open an offshore bank account. One way is to go to the chosen country and visit the bank personally. And as far as most bankers are concerned, this is the preferred method. A number of foreign countries are now requiring that new customers appear in person to open accounts. The reason given is that bankers should know their customers so that they don't do business with drug merchants, terrorists, and crooked politicians. You might be able to open the account by mail, depending on the bank's rules.

Most offshore banks allow you to conduct transactions by mail, fax, or telex (and some are slowly adopting the Internet, but most good banks abroad are still very wary of online transactions). But you might not be able to use these methods to open the account.

Privacy Concerns

The question that concerns many Americans is how to transfer their money to the account. You may, of course, simply write a check against your U.S. bank account or money market account. But if privacy is a reason for opening the account, writing a check against a not very private account defeats your purpose.

Reporting Cash Payments

Under U.S. law, it is illegal to move $10,000 or more in cash (or cash equivalents) out of the country without filing the appropriate form—usually IRS Form 4789 or Customs Service Form 4790. The law also applies to traveler's checks, bearer bonds, and other securities negotiable either in the United States or abroad. U.S. banks making out a draft or a wire transfer on your behalf must also file the appropriate form. The maximum penalty for failure to do so is five years in jail and a fine of $500,000. It used to be that the simplest way legally to avoid creating an official record of your across-the-border transactions was to limit them to sizes of less than $10,000, but new legislation on money laundering prohibits structuring transactions to avoid the reporting. This law has stronger teeth than the reporting law itself, and a money-laundering conviction can result in a 20-year prison sentence and forfeiture of all of your property. And forget probation for first offenders. It not only doesn't exist any more, but federal judges are required to give the mandatory prison sentences specified in the laundering statute—the judge no longer has discretion in setting the sentence.

Remember, you can be guilty of laundering your own money—this isn't just a crime committed by a broker handling drug dealers' money for a fee. There have already been several convictions for money laundering of what would otherwise have been perfectly normal, legitimate transactions.

One was the man who borrowed against his house, took the money in cash, and then made several separate cash deposits to his son's college account. Nothing wrong in the purpose, but the account was forfeited and he was convicted of a structured transaction to avoid reporting. Motive is irrelevant and was never even mentioned in the court case.

WIRE TRANSFER WATCH

As required by federal regulations, a system of recording wire transfers operates in U.S. banks. These movements of funds are normally used when speed is of the essence. Because banks themselves guarantee the fund's availability, wire transfers are accepted as cash. Of course, those asking their banks to wire money must pay a fee for the privilege. Thanks to these regulations, banks are now required to maintain extensive paperwork documenting the transfer. Of course, this means that domestic wire-transfer costs to the banks have gone up. The result is that many account holders have realized that these services cost more. In effect, all users of wire transfers are being penalized so that the government, in its effort to crack down on drugs, can better record the movement of money between bank accounts.

INTERNATIONAL TRANSFERS

When regulations and procedures are in place (they are slowly being implemented), the same kind of surveillance will be introduced internationally. At present, only U.S. banks can be obliged by the authorities in this country to maintain such records. Foreign banks, regulated by their own authorities, are under no obligation to inform U.S. bank examiners of the ownership of accounts they hold. The result is that increased information is available only on Americans who send money overseas. Still, no one is able to determine to whom such transfers go or what they were for. Nor is anyone tracking wire transfers originating outside the United States—yet. But today the majority of countries have their own reporting rules, and there are extensive networks of treaties (usually mutual legal assistance treaties) providing for the sharing of information between governments.

In some ways a simple personal check is better than it might seem at first. True, it leaves a trail to your account, but it is not automatically reported by anyone, with all the problems that creates. Or you can simply open a separate personal or business account on which to draw the checks sent abroad. As a bonus, if you close the account after you are done with the transactions and the account was in a distant state to start with, the account records go into the bank's dead file instead of the active computer and eventually get destroyed. Money-market accounts with checking privileges also work extremely well for this purpose. You write a check from your personal account to the money-market fund, use one of its checks to send the money abroad, and then close the money-market account. This is clearly legal and avoids any issue of what is or is not structuring with money orders. The paper trail does exist, but it takes a massive amount of work to follow it.

REPORTING FOREIGN BANK ACCOUNTS

Another law covers foreign bank accounts. It requires Americans to report ownership of non-U.S. bank accounts valued at $10,000 or more. You have no reporting requirement as long as the per-person total in all foreign bank accounts does not exceed $10,000 at any point in a tax year. That means every member of a family can have his or her own foreign account. This threshold applies to the sum of all accounts plus certificates of deposit. It also includes the cash and negotiable securities in securities accounts. The penalties for not complying are the same as those for illegally exporting funds but not as severe as the new money-laundering penalties.

Here, also, the simplest way to avoid the reporting

requirement legally is to make sure that your balance remains below $10,000. However, that may be more difficult than it seems: uncertainties arise in calculating the exchange rate you must use in converting the deutsche marks or the yen in your account.

Unfortunately, you cannot use the exchange rate printed in the financial section of the newspaper. You must use the official rates calculated by the Federal Reserve Bank of New York. The problem is that those rates are not released until well after the year is over. By the time you find out what exchange rate the government will use to value your account, it is too late to make any downward adjustments in your balance.

The only solution to this problem is to leave yourself a conservative margin by staying well below the reporting threshold. If your account approaches the limit, transfer some money to your spouse or your children. If a foreign currency appreciates against the dollar and you earn interest besides, you may have to reduce your overseas holdings to stay under the ceiling.

Investing to Stay under the Minimum

Another thing you can do is invest some of your balance. The $10,000 ceiling does not apply to foreign stocks, bonds, mutual funds, and investment funds that you may own—as long as they are not in a foreign securities account or a foreign bank account. A securities account includes a brokerage account and such things as a foreign bank acting as securities custodian. It is not inconceivable that a foreign accountant or lawyer holding securities as your nominee could be deemed a securities account, and you probably don't want to be the first test case.

If you are in danger of hitting the ceiling, buy a bond or a mutual fund and take delivery of the certificate. It can be sent by registered mail to your address in the United States, or it can be sent to an officer of an overseas bank, who will accept it on your behalf and hold it until you can pick it up at some future date. As long as it needs your physical endorsement to be negotiated, that temporary holding is probably not a securities account.

Put the bond or stock certificate in a safe deposit box and then it won't be in a securities account. This strategem will not work with most foreign mutual funds because most of them do not issue certificates, but a direct fund holding registered in your name is a shareholding, not a securities account.

In addition, many countries have eliminated the issue of stock and bond certificates entirely. You cannot take delivery because the securities exist only in book entry form. Many countries in Europe are moving toward paperless securities in book entry form. This distinction between securities inside and outside an account results from the U.S. government's mistaken premise that any negotiable instrument in a securities account is as liquid as cash.

EXPATRIATE VIOLATION

In practice, Americans living overseas are the most frequent violators of the reporting requirement. Thousands of them exceed the $10,000 threshold at some time or another. Moreover, overseas IRS offices do not routinely inform Americans about the reporting rules. But with the new emphasis in this area, you might find your passport revoked or not renewed, forcing you back to the United States to stand trial.

TAX CONCERNS

As a U.S. citizen, you are taxed by the United States on your worldwide income. This includes interest and other income earned by the offshore bank account. That's not a big problem, and you probably are prepared for it. Don't fall for the argument some promoters make that you can open the account, let interest accumulate for a few years, and then spend the income tax free overseas. If the IRS finds out about this, it can prosecute you for tax fraud.

The interest earned on the foreign account probably will be paid or credited to you in a foreign currency. For tax purposes, you have to value it in U.S. dollars, using one of two exchange rates. If you bring the money back to the United States, you use the rate that prevails at the time of the transfer. If you do not bring the money back, you use the official exchange rate calculated by the New York Federal Reserve Bank.

AVOIDING DOUBLE TAXATION

Be aware that a foreign government with jurisdiction over your non-U.S. bank may impose its own withholding taxes. Switzerland, for example, withholds 35 percent of your interest earnings at the source. If the country in question has a double-taxation treaty with the United States, you may qualify for a deduction on your U.S. return, but then you also have to declare the existence of your bank account. (The amount you can recover varies from country to country according to the terms of whatever treaty is in force at the time. However, you are unlikely to recover more than a fraction of what was withheld in the first place.)

SELECTING A BANK

The bank you choose depends upon your goals. If you want maximum privacy and protection from the U.S. government, the courts, and anyone who might win a court judgment against you, you do not want to use an offshore bank that has branches or subsidiaries in the United States. The U.S. courts have been known to threaten the demise of such branches or subsidiaries if the offshore parent company does not comply with U.S. orders. But if you want an easy and fast way to set up an offshore account, you want to use a foreign bank that has U.S. branches, or you might want to use a major

U.S. bank that has foreign offices or subsidiaries. This allows you to walk into a U.S. office and have that office assist you in setting up the offshore account.

You probably also want to check the fees at several banks before selecting one. In a number of countries, banking fees can be rather expensive, far more than what many Americans are used to paying. Any investment and tax advantages of the offshore account might be seriously diminished by high fees.

GETTING YOUR MONEY OUT

If you are using your haven account only to trade international stocks, getting your money out of this account is no different than making a withdrawal from your local bank. You merely request a check in the currency of your choice and deposit it wherever you like.

If financial privacy is your concern, you don't want a haven account check with your name on it floating around the U.S. or Canadian banking system. It leaves an audit trail that will reveal your secret.

The easiest way to avoid such a trail is to restrict yourself to cash withdrawals in person. Traditionally, a more convenient course is to inquire whether your haven bank can issue you a VISA or American Express card. When the bill for your charges on such a card is presented to your bank, it is paid out of your account. But in 2000 this practice came under assault when the U.S. government won a court case upholding a request that MasterCard provide copies of all U.S. purchases made with Caribbean-issued credit cards. While this is a long way from being able to link those transactions to U.S. account holders, it is symptomatic of the trend we are seeing in enforcement. Once again, my point that seeking total secrecy with an assumption that one won't get caught is not the way to go, and there is no point in committing serious felonies (each purchase may eventually be listed as a separate offense) when there are enough perfectly legal things that can be done.

THE ULTIMATE OFFSHORE BANK LOOPHOLE

Suppose you don't want to simply open a foreign bank account. Suppose you want to bank offshore, but you want some more control of your money. One option a number of Americans have proposed is ownership of an offshore bank.

Owning a bank is a lot easier in many countries than it is in the United States. Some countries cater to individual foreigners who want to own banks, streamlining chartering rules and making the cost an affordable $20,000 or so.

Many people who have opened their own offshore banks have improperly used the banks to defraud others or to evade their taxes. Banking havens take precautions to ensure that you, as bank-owning foreigners, do not conduct any banking business with their citizens.

But that doesn't mean you have to use the bank improperly. It can be a real bank with a genuine charter, capable of joining the world of international banking. It can take deposits, make loans, issue letters of credit, and invest money.

Here's the best part for U.S. citizens: offshore banking income is not presently considered subpart F income. When an offshore corporation is controlled by U.S. citizens, the subpart F income passes through to the U.S. shareholders as though it were a partnership. But banking income is not subpart F income. The profits accumulate in the offshore bank and are compounded free of U.S. taxes. If you set up the bank in the right country, your taxes will be low in your home country. Careful investing and use of tax treaties should eliminate or reduce taxes from any other country.

To qualify for the exception from subpart F, your bank must conduct real business. This means that you have to solicit business from independent parties, and you have to get deposits and make loans. If the parties involved are not independent of the bank's owners, the IRS likely will say that it is simply an offshore investment corporation and not a bank and will tax U.S. shareholders on the corporation's income.

To start a foreign bank properly, you need at least $250,000 in startup capital. You also need professional advice to select the right country for incorporation and to find someone to manage the bank in that country. One of the real advantages of an offshore bank is that you do not need a walk-in retail operation, such as that of your neighborhood bank. Most offshore banking transactions are done through modern electronic communications. The occasional client who wants to visit the bank will be satisfied with an office that looks like any other professional office.

Because of its attacks on drug dealers and their financial operations, the United States is constantly lobbying countries with liberal banking rules to change them. Therefore, many of the Caribbean countries that used to be ideal for setting up private offshore banks are now fairly inconvenient to use. They require more startup capital than formerly, and they might not even want to give you a charter. But if you are serious about operating an offshore bank and if you seek help from someone who is up on the international banking situation, you might find that the private offshore bank is the ultimate offshore loophole.

AN OFFSHORE HAVEN IS NOT NECESSARILY THE BEST PLACE TO BANK

If you don't think of major industrialized countries as secrecy havens, you are overlooking a valuable strategy. Rather than doing your banking in an attention-attracting haven like the Bahamas or the Cayman Islands, there is much to be said for quietly opening a normal account in almost any country outside the United States. Most all respect privacy more than the United States does, and your dealings with the bank will not be particularly noteworthy. Every country has lots of American residents who open bank accounts for one reason or another. If you create your own privacy haven in this way instead of joining the crowd writing to the latest bank touted in a privacy newsletter, you will be much better off. Very few countries (with the exception of Switzerland) tax the bank accounts of nonresidents. Even the United States does not tax foreigner's bank accounts in this country. Choose a country because of family or business ties, and you have another reason for the particular account that helps it to blend in. On this basis, lots of places are practical: Germany, France, Belgium, the Netherlands, Argentina, Mexico, Australia, Singapore . . . you get the idea.

Chapter 6

Prudent Ways for Americans to Buy Offshore Funds

ventually one needs to make a direct foreign investment. Buying U.S.-based global or international mutual funds is a useful currency diversification and a helpful way for the smaller investor to get started. But since these funds are still a U.S. asset, such fund investments do not help to diversify your assets in an asset-protection sense, safeguarding against lawsuits, forfeitures, possible future exchange controls, or any other contingencies.

It is not illegal for Americans to buy offshore mutual funds (called unit trusts in some countries) or any other security that is not registered for sale in the United States. Most foreign securities that are not mutual funds can be bought through any good stockbroker, although you can do better if you select a broker who specializes in foreign securities. But he can't sell you a foreign mutual fund. That doesn't mean that there is something dirty or illegal about it; it merely means that the fund is not registered for sale in the United States.

There are a number of reasons for this. Expense is one; successful foreign funds don't need the U.S. market and see little reason to pay the outrageous fees of our litigious society. (Some of the best foreign cars cannot be purchased in the U.S. for a similar reason. The makers of $100,000 custom cars are not about to give the federal government 10 free cars per year for destruction testing.) Some of the funds cannot meet U.S. legal requirements because they charge investors a performance fee rather than a management fee based on a percentage of assets. But many investors would actually prefer a fund manager whose only compensation is a share of the profits instead of a fee based on the total investments in the fund. The manager's goals are different.

It is illegal for a foreign securities issuer, such as a mutual fund, to sell an unregistered security in the United States. To be completely safe, most (but not all) of them refuse to sell to a U.S. citizen or resident even if he is residing abroad. They'd rather stay away from anything to do with Americans. To protect themselves, they require a statement on the application that the purchaser is not a resident or citizen of the United States.

Some advisors suggest using a mail-forwarding service in a foreign country and simply signing a false declaration. It may be quite safe to do so, but such dishonesty could turn out to be imprudent later. To take an extreme example (at least we hope it is an extreme example), some other country could suddenly adopt U.S.–style forfeiture laws and decide that securities procured by fraud were forfeit to the government. (The false declaration is clearly a fraudulent statement, even if there is no financial loss to the seller.)

This example might seem extreme, but a recent U.S. case presents a scary analogy. A mortgage applicant in 1986 made an allegedly false statement about his employment. In 1992, the federal government confiscated the house on the grounds that the false employment statement was fraud on a federally insured bank, even though the mortgage had been paid. The householder claimed that he had worked for the company off the books, but payroll records did not support his claim. The U.S. Court of Appeals ruled in 1993 that the house was subject to administrative forfeiture by the government and that the owner was not entitled to a hearing or trial or to present his defense to a court.

Looked at in another way, although the purchase of the securities by an American is not illegal, it would not be impossible for the U.S. government to argue that the securities are subject to forfeiture on the grounds that the purchaser committed mail fraud by mailing a false declaration of citizenship. The U.S. Supreme Court has long ruled that mail fraud need not involve a monetary loss, but only the mailing of a false statement with an intangible gain (in this example, the ownership of a security that could not have been obtained without the false statement). Thus all the legal elements of proof for a mail-fraud case would have been met. More likely than a mail-fraud prosecution, however, would be a civil forfeiture of the security, similar to the mortgage example above. And why contaminate an honest investment by taking even the slightest risk of acquiring it in an illegal manner? There is no reason to do so when the entire transaction can be conducted honestly, legally, and properly.

These horror stories may seem far-fetched examples, but the house-seizure case suggests that they may not be.

So how can an American purchase these securities legally? There are two possible routes that meet the legal requirements.

The first is to use a foreign bank or trust company as a nominee holder. In this example, the nominee holds the security under a simple agreement for the true owner. This is technically a form of trust but is normally limited to a one- or two-paragraph standard agreement form used by the bank. This strategy would not be valid if the form required by the offshore fund included a statement that the beneficial owner is not an American. Most of these fund statements do not go that far, but some do (in particular the Fidelity Group offshore-based funds) because they are part of a U.S. parent company.

The second strategy is a more sophisticated version of the first. A simple trust is created, with the foreign bank or trust company acting as trustee and the beneficiary being the U.S. holder, with a spouse and/or offspring being contingent beneficiaries in case of death. Now the trust itself is the legal and the beneficial owner, and the requirements of the fund have been met. The fact that the trust has American beneficiaries is not legally the same as the shares being beneficially owned by an American.

Such agreements are usually simple, and most major foreign banks can deal with them. For example, banks in Canada, Britain, and Hong Kong will usually charge only around $500 to set up a trust and around $50 or $100 per year per security for nominee agreements. A Swiss bank can also act as a nominee.

Canada and Britain are mentioned in the example for a reason: it is not necessary to go to a tax haven for this kind of service. Very few countries are interested in taxing a trust in which the assets and the beneficiaries are foreign, so even a high-tax country will usually qualify for this type of simple trust or nominee arrangement. The bank will be able to tell you the local tax position for such an arrangement.

New Zealand has become particularly useful for such arrangements because its tax laws clearly state that a nonresident beneficiary and his trust are not subject to New Zealand tax on non–New Zealand assets.

The banks in the high-tax countries tend to be far cheaper— this is as routine as asking your local bank's trust department to hold a share certificate for your children—and you avoid the high trust formation fees that most tax havens charge.

In theory a Swiss bank could be a trustee rather than a nominee, but this gets into some exotic legal questions of civil versus common-law countries because the IRS will only recognize a common-law trust. In the chapter on Swiss resources we'll examine even better opportunities offered by Swiss institutions that provide a complete fund management service as well as holding the investments.

By using either of the approaches outlined and staying in a common-law country—Britain and the countries that inherited the British legal system (e.g., the United States)— the trust is neutral or transparent for tax purposes. The value of this is that you can then claim a U.S. tax credit for any foreign withholding taxes paid by the trust, although normally the point of offshore funds is that there are no withholding taxes.

On January 1, 2001, the United States imposed new withholding tax regulations on remittance of interest, dividends, and capital gains to foreign (offshore) banks and brokers. The foreign bank or broker holding the account of a U.S. taxpayer will supply this form and invite the clients to authorize disclosure/nondisclosure to the IRS of their bank relationship. Noncomplying U.S. taxpayers can no longer trade U.S. domestic securities through foreign accounts because the U.S. withholding tax of 31 percent on sales proceeds (not only gains) would be deducted. This includes U.S. money market paper, Treasury bills, and domestic bonds. On interest and dividends earned on U.S. domestic paper, 30 percent will be deducted. Foreign securities and a range of international mutual funds (both U.S. dollar or foreign currency denominated) are exempt, even though they may be holding U.S. equities or debt instruments.

A U.S. taxpayer, as defined under U.S. laws (e.g., a citizen, resident, green card holder, foreign spouse of a U.S. citizen, or anyone who must file a U.S. tax return) is restricted from owning U.S. domestic securities through a foreign bank or broker unless IRS Form W-9 is completed. The regulation does not cover foreign securities held by Americans, but it may be the beginning of a trend. Different banks are dealing with it in different ways—some are closing all accounts for Americans; some are requiring account holders to make a choice between signing a secrecy waiver or disposing of all U.S. securities in the account; others are still confused, and some have mistakenly reported all securities, not just U.S. securities.

Swiss banks DO NOT automatically disclose any information whatsoever to the IRS or to anybody at all unless specifically authorized to do so in writing by the client.

Unfortunately, these worldwide policing and exchange of information trends are only likely to get worse in coming years, and it is important to think ahead rather than to just react. For that reason, among others, much time in this book will be devoted to exploring ways to truly internationalize your life and your assets instead of just relying on the traditional ways of going offshore.

Chapter 7

Offshore Corporations and Trusts

ffshore corporations can be set up worldwide for a variety of purposes, including the holding and management of assets, international trading, manufacturing and marketing activities, and tax reduction. Both tangible assets (e.g., cash and real estate) and intangible assets (e.g., patents, copyrights, trademarks) may be held by corporations. Corporations formed specifically for the purpose of holding intangible assets are especially useful for quickly and economically transferring these assets from owner to owner. Instead of having to sell patent or trademark rights, for example, buyers merely acquire the shares of the existing corporation and all the assets it holds. Active entrepreneurs can establish several separate corporations to help manage different assets or personal needs.

Corporations are treated as legal entities, in a sense *artificial people* in the eyes of the law. Because the corporation is not merely a collection of individuals, but rather a legally recognized entity on its own merit, it may afford shareholders protection against liabilities arising from its operations. It can sue and be sued, but the individual owners are usually shielded against losses beyond their shareholdings in the corporation. Owners of unincorporated businesses, on the other hand, can lose their own personal assets in the event of successful suits by creditors. Assets including cash, securities, homes, and cars are at risk even if they are totally unrelated to the business conducted by the individual. Under the law, it is impossible to separate the business assets of a sole proprietorship from the personal assets of the business owner. A creditor who goes after a proprietor soon proceeds to seize personal as well as business assets in satisfaction of any judgments.

Although domestic corporations provide protection for individual shareholders against such *personal* seizures, they still leave shareholders open to litigation against the corporation itself. Corporate assets including cash holdings, bank deposits, office equipment, and accounts receivable are still at risk. The foreign corporation offers significantly more protection because assets can be kept out of public view. Its owners can often remain completely anonymous, and judgments obtained in one country may be difficult if not impossible to enforce in another country where the business is incorporated.

Foreign corporations may also convey benefits analogous to foreign citizenship, providing trade advantages not available to outsiders. By establishing a corporation in a particular jurisdiction, entrepreneurs can often take advantage of reduced trade tariffs and barriers.

People sometimes talk about corporate shells, which can either be established from scratch or purchased. The term *shell* merely implies that a corporate structure exists with no current activity taking place. However, the shell, a corporation chartered by the local jurisdiction, is every bit as legal as a major multinational corporation doing billions of dollars of business. It can be formed by local incorporators, have as few as one owner and director, and exist with virtually no assets. It need not have an office or a staff. It can operate out of the desk drawer of its appointed service agent. To simplify and speed the process of incorporating, some people choose to buy already chartered corporate shells that were set up specifically for the purpose of being sold and operated by new owners.

For many, the offshore corporation's primary benefit is privacy or anonymity. The corporation's name need not have any relationship to your own name; indeed, you can usually select any name you wish for your corporation as long as it has not already been taken by another incorporated entity in the same jurisdiction. An offshore corporation allows an investor or entrepreneur to conduct business activities in a manner that makes it difficult for potential creditors or poachers to cause financial damage.

The choice of offshore corporate locations should be predicated on several factors. Cost is naturally one of them. Generally speaking, offshore corporations can be quickly chartered with the help of local counsel for less than $3,000. In some instances, costs can be as low as $575. All jurisdictions require that a local agent be named solely for the service of process; the agent receives an annual fee. The government issuing the corporate charter will also charge an annual franchise fee or tax. Together, these maintenance fees might cost the corporation another $500 to $1,000 annually.

Before setting up a foreign corporation, you should also consider the relative political stabilities of the competing choices. A nation that is stable and neutral is likely to provide a better environment for international trading than one with many enemies. It is also important to find a jurisdiction whose courts are friendly to its corporations in the event of lawsuits. Perhaps most important, corporate domiciles that guarantee confidentiality and at the same time minimize reporting requirements should be favored. The establishment of an offshore corporation should not bring with it a torrent of filing and regulatory requirements.

In setting up an offshore corporation, it is important to consult with an advisor who understands the benefits, limitations, and intricacies inherent in such ventures.

One consulting business specializing in the formation of offshore corporations and trusts is Britannia Corporate Management Limited, located in the Cayman Islands. Its president, Gary F. Oakley, is a Canadian with 17 years of Cayman Islands residency. Britannia is licensed to manage investment-holding and -trading companies, real estate–holding companies, patent-holding companies, and insurance-holding companies. It is licensed to incorporate and manage corporations registered in the Cayman Islands. As such, the firm can serve as the registered office of a corporation; provide its secretary, officers, and directors; or undertake any day-to-day functions that may be required. More information can be obtained by writing the following:

Britannia Corporate Management Limited
Attn: New Clients Information
P. O. Box 1968
Whitewall Estates, Grand Cayman
Cayman Islands

Britannia can be reached by fax at +1 345 949 0716, marking your fax "New Clients Information."

FOREIGN CORPORATE BANK ACCOUNTS

If your corporation intends to do business internationally, it will undoubtedly want to maintain an account with a strong and reputable foreign bank. Even the largest multinational banks that maintain offices in foreign jurisdictions are bound by local laws and customs. The clear advantage of banking with larger institutions is protection against bank failure because they are well capitalized and their risks are spread widely. When dealing with smaller banks, local investor protection programs may be inadequate for your corporation's needs. Insurance is often afforded only for modest deposits and then sometimes only in local currencies.

Also consider, however, that greater privacy is sometimes achieved in dealing with smaller but well-capitalized banks whose records are maintained locally. An added bonus of dealing with smaller local banks is that they are often more autonomous, allowing them to make loans, accept letters of credit, and make other financial decisions quickly and with less red tape.

It is important to ask about a bank's international finance experience—its ability to routinely process letters of credit and deal with multicurrency and cross-border issues. Make certain that the bank you select can handle instructions by fax or phone if that is what you require. Many offshore banks will not honor such requests. Finally, you will undoubtedly want to work with a bank whose employees are fluent in your native language.

Corporations can change the names of signatories (the people it authorizes to make deposits and withdrawals) at any time. This is done by a simple corporate resolution, signed by the directors, and presented to the chosen bank. Computerized records at such banks tend to reflect corporate account names rather than personal signatories, adding another layer of confidentiality should prying eyes gain access to bank records. Anyone on a hunting expedition trying to find you will not routinely come across your name in the course of a search. Bear in mind that most foreign laws also provide stronger protection against the arbitrary release of bank records anyway, so disclosure is highly unlikely in any event.

OFFSHORE TRUSTS

Although corporations have to be owned by other entities—either individuals or other corporations—trusts in effect own themselves. The distinction is important when you consider the tax consequences of corporations and trusts. Corporate shareholders are generally responsible for paying income taxes on distributions made to them by their corporations as dividends. Both profits from operations and capital gains are taxable during the course of a corporation's life or upon its liquidation. The corporation may itself pay corporate taxes on all of its profits, before dividends are distributed to shareholders, giving rise to the expression *double taxation*.

The trust, like the corporation, is considered a separate legal entity. The trust is a legal device that allows title and possession of property to be held by one person, the *trustee*, for the benefit of one or more other persons, the *beneficiaries*. A trust can hold title to virtually any type of assets. It can conduct business much like a corporation. It can be used to dole out money to the elderly or pay medical or education bills. One of the major benefits of the trust is that it can streamline inheritance processes, avoiding the costly and time-consuming hurdles of probate.

Unlike the corporation, however, the trust has no outside owners to whom taxing authorities can look for money. A *grantor* creates and funds the trust, determining the rules by which the trust will operate, legally called the *declaration*. The powers granted to the trustee may be very broad or more narrowly defined. They control the way the trustee manages the trust's assets during the grantor's life and after his death. One or more *beneficiaries* are named by the grantor; they receive distributions as provided in the trust's guidelines. The day-to-day operations of the trust are placed in the hands of a trustee who decides, within the guidelines originally established, how assets are to be prudently invested and distributed. Banks, trust companies, and other specially trained financial advisors are often appointed as trustees.

Although a single individual can theoretically take on all three roles—grantor, beneficiary, and trustee—such a trust will normally provide little or no asset protection or tax relief.

This is also true of domestic revocable trusts in which the grantor reserves the right to terminate the trust at any time and regain the assets.

Offshore trusts can provide significant measures of both asset protection and privacy. The names of grantors and beneficiaries need not be a matter of public record. Nonetheless, if you appoint yourself as beneficiary of the offshore trust, tax authorities at home may take the position that because you continue to benefit from the trust, its assets should remain at risk in the event a creditor goes after them. You can limit this liability by establishing a trust in which you are given a beneficial interest in the income generated by the trust but not the initial capital placed in the trust. A much safer approach is to remain at arm's length from your trust, naming family members as beneficiaries.

For the same reason, it is best to appoint an independent trustee to manage the trust's day-to-day operations. In determining whether a trust has a legitimate purpose, something other than mere tax avoidance, a court at home is likely to consider the degree to which you have distanced yourself from the trust. Offshore trustees are of course not bound by rulings of courts or administrative bodies in your home country, providing further protection against creditors, forfeitures, and seizures. The trustee should be selected carefully, knowing that you are placing in his hands the control of your valuable assets.

In some foreign countries, the grantor may also name a *protector* for the trust, an individual who oversees the trustee. A protector has the power to fire and replace the trustee if he believes the trust is not being managed in accordance with the rules originally set out. The grantor can serve as protector, but in the event of a dispute in a home court such an arrangement might again raise red flags about the degree to which the trust has been operated independently of those with a beneficial interest.

Offshore trusts are frequently used for international investment purposes. Although the foreign trustee makes actual investments of assets within the trust, you can certainly participate by phone or letter in suggesting particular strategies or investment vehicles. Privacy and confidentiality are ensured, domestic reporting requirements are drastically reduced, taxes are avoided, diversification is achieved, and financial flexibility is greatly enhanced.

Switzerland is often selected as a venue for the management of trusts for all the reasons outlined in an earlier chapter. Swiss law provides investors with most of the tools necessary to ensure secrecy, promote capital preservation, protect against creditors, and reduce tax liabilities. But Switzerland is a civil law country and does not have trusts itself. Swiss asset managers will provide the investment administration for a trust created under the laws of another country, such as in the Cayman Islands or the Isle of Man.

In creating a trust, it is exceedingly important to select a country and an advisor wisely. Bogus trusts that purport to take title and possession of assets but that have clearly been set up solely for the purpose of defrauding creditors often prove worthless. In many instances, physical assets remain in the home country, perhaps in banks or brokerage houses. In the United States, federal and state courts frequently declare such trusts to be shams and accordingly order the seizure of such assets to pay creditors. The maintenance of a *paper trust*, often created at significant cost by a trust mill, offers no real protection.

"If something is too good to be true it usually is" applies especially to offshore trusts. There are numerous U.S. promoters selling tax-free offshore trust packages, telling their clients that this magic bullet will legally exempt them from U.S. income taxes. It is not true. This is purely and simply a fraud, but since *you*, not the promoter, are the one who is going to cheat on taxes, it is *you*, not the promoter, who is going to go to prison. Legitimate offshore trusts are a very complex matter and need to be carefully set up with proper professional advice to achieve their objectives.

Promoters of phony offshore trust schemes often bolster

their sales materials with documents that purport to be legal opinions but are no such thing. A legal opinion is a letter given to you by a lawyer, after a proper consultation about your circumstances, advising you about the law on a proposed transaction. What these promoters usually hand out is a paper with citations from various cases and quotations from the U.S. Constitution, the Internal Revenue Code, and other authorities upon which they say the unsuspecting taxpayer can rely. It is neither a legal opinion, nor is it legal. It is rubbish.

Some of these trusts provide the client with a debit card good at automatic teller machines. That is clearly impossible in a legitimate trust, since it undermines the role of the trust and would let the beneficiary make withdrawals at any time. That converts the whole thing from a trust to a sham, and the courts get very nasty about shams.

Recently, the United States has obtained convictions of some of these promoters on charges of conspiracy to defraud the United States by impeding the IRS and conspiracy to evade federal income taxes. The convictions have been based on the promoters' participation in schemes to assist their clients in reducing or evading federal income taxes by forming sham trusts.

When an abusive trust arrangement is identified by the IRS the participants will pay deficiencies, interest, maximum penalties, and significant attorneys' and accountants' fees to fix a situation that never should have happened. At least the lucky participants will—the unlucky participants will be going to prison, and that solution seems to be on the increase lately.

THE HYBRID COMPANY

An interesting alternative to the trust is something called the *hybrid company*, a structure available today in the Isle of Man. This type of arrangement evolved because English law never provided for the formation of nonprofit corporations.

Instead, ordinary companies were formed with members agreeing to guarantee the debts incurred by their organizations in small, finite amounts. In reality, this is analogous to the manner in which U.S. corporate shareholders guarantee the debts of their corporations to the extent of their individual stock investments.

The hybrid company combines a guarantee company with a more traditional share-issuing company under a single umbrella. Today, hybrid companies serve the needs of wealthy investors in situations where regular trusts are too restrictive or are unavailable for a variety of reasons. Hybrid companies can operate as quasi-trusts or what has been called *incorporated trusts*, providing the same benefits as conventional trusts under a somewhat more complex organizational design.

People living in civil law jurisdictions where the typical Anglo-Saxon trust is not understood or recognized by their governments can make good use of the corporate trust structure created by the hybrid company. Civil code countries may recognize trusts created outside their borders, but not when created by their own residents. The same rule of thumb applies to common-law countries; they will recognize trusts only to the extent that they are created by individuals whose own domiciles recognize such trusts.

In still other countries, individuals may not normally be given the option of choosing their heirs, their governments instead determining who inherits the estates of decedents. In these situations, hybrid company trusts ensure that estates are disposed of according to the wishes of their owners.

Corporations are generally recognized universally and accepted, even in those jurisdictions that do not recognize trusts. The hybrid company, a vehicle with a corporate structure, thus provides a recognized means of separating the legal ownership of assets from those with a beneficial interest in them. A shareholding member of the hybrid company may retain control of assets but may not benefit from them. In this capacity, he can protect the assets against the future threats of creditors. Guarantee members, on the other hand, are analogous to beneficiaries of a trust. They are legally considered guarantors, not shareholders, and are thus not required to disclose their interest in the trust, which provides significant anonymity.

When a guarantee member dies, his membership ends much as a partner's membership ends in a partnership upon his death. Membership does not pass to family or heirs on death, nor can it be transferred during his lifetime. New guarantee members can instead be elected to fill the void.

The relationship between shareholding member and guarantee member enables the hybrid company to function as a trust. A shareholding member normally has the right to income and assets upon the termination of a company, generally in proportion to the capital contributed to the company during its life. A guarantee member does not normally contribute capital; he only pays in an agreed-upon amount necessary to guarantee debts of the company. He may or may not have rights upon liquidation, depending on the terms of the articles of association, the governing rules of the hybrid company.

When used for trust purposes, the hybrid company's management is placed in the hands of shareholding members and directors. They are prohibited from receiving any financial distributions. Guarantee members, on the other hand, receive dividends and can avail themselves of other benefits such as low-interest loans. They do not actively participate in the company's decisionmaking process and generally do not vote in elections. In effect, they become beneficiaries of the trust that has been created.

Individuals as well as charitable organizations and family foundations can benefit immensely from the asset protection, privacy, and tax advantages of the hybrid company. Arrangements are very complex, however, and should only be undertaken by an advisor fully skilled in this structure. Americans are especially cautioned to make certain that the requirements of the IRS are met to avoid later difficulties.

The foremost expert in hybrid companies is Skye Fiduciary Services Limited. Under the direction of its chairman, Charles Cain (formerly managing director of the second merchant bank to open in the Isle of Man), Skye Fiduciary is the most experienced offshore corporate and trust management business in the jurisdiction. Although Skye offers a full range of company and trust management services, its expertise in designing novel company structures to meet the needs of foreign clients is unique.

For further information, write the following:

Skye Fiduciary Services Limited
Attn: New Clients Department
2 Water Street
Ramsey, Isle of Man 1M8 1JP
United Kingdom

The telephone number is +44 1624 816117. Fax service is available at +44 1624 816645 (from most parts of the United States, you need to dial 011 before the phone numbers given). Direct communications to New Clients Information.

Chapter 8

Offshore Privacy:
Issues Beyond Banking

The chairman of an up-an-coming publicly traded U.S. corporation was recently diagnosed with prostate cancer. Fortunately, his malignancy was of a type and at a stage with an excellent prognosis for full recovery. Knowing how sensitive stockholders are to the health of their leaders, on whom they depend for management guidance, the CEO carefully arranged to take a couple of weeks of vacation. He quietly checked into a hospital a few hundred miles from his company's executive offices for the required treatment, hoping to keep himself out of the limelight.

These precautions proved inadequate. Within days of his hospital admission, word of the illness leaked out into the business and investment communities. His company's stock plummeted almost 20 percent, reducing the corporation's equity by millions of dollars. Some individual shareholders, including the chairman himself, lost tens and in some cases hundreds of thousands of dollars. Rumors, whether founded or not, can be economically devastating for individuals as well as their businesses.

MEDICAL RECORDS PRIVACY

There are many reasons to shield your medical records from public scrutiny. The mere fact that you have had an illness, even when it has been completely controlled or cured, can cost you and your family millions of dollars. Despite the supposed protections of law, health problems routinely result in the denial or loss of employment, the cancellation or loss of insurance benefits, and serious economic losses such as those suffered by the CEO just discussed.

A business executive with an illness perceived to be life threatening becomes a pariah in the eyes of his colleagues. A sports figure with a potentially disabling illness or injury finds himself put out to pasture. An actress with drug or alcohol problems falls from the good graces of casting executives and producers. A law enforcement officer or fire fighter who develops mildly elevated blood pressure finds himself out of work even though the condition is completely controllable with medication.

Despite canons of ethics that require that physicians, hospitals, and other health care providers maintain patient records in strict confidence, information leaks are rampant in the United States. It is easy to find out whether someone you know has been hospitalized. Just call the hospital's desk and ask for the room number of someone you suspect is a patient. In seconds, your suspicions will be confirmed. Home in on an innocent breakfast conversation among nurses who have just left their facility; you are likely to hear shop talk about difficult patients they have cared for during the night.

If you followed the trial of the Menendez brothers in California for murdering their parents, you know that a psychiatrist who provided therapy for the pair testified about their alleged confession at their criminal trial, and so did the psychiatrist's girlfriend who admitted spying on the doctor and his clients. What was once believed to be privileged medical information isn't so privileged anymore. Sometimes information leaks from health-care facilities are far more benign but nonetheless potentially damaging. When an envelope-stuffing machine recently went haywire in Florida, one customer of a large clinical laboratory received the itemized bills of several dozen other clients whose patient numbers happened to follow his own. The paperwork included diagnosis codes, lists of tests run by the laboratory, and even the names of all the referring physicians and their insurance companies.

Then there is the problem of medical reporting. The Medical Information Bureau as well as other repositories of information maintain computerized files on millions of Americans with no guarantee that the information is even vaguely correct. Like credit-reporting agencies, these bureaus collect millions of pieces of data annually and then redistribute the information to insurers, employers, and others keen on invading your privacy.

Suppose you go to your physician for a routine physical examination. A nurse attempts to draw blood for routine analysis but has difficulty obtaining an adequate sample, so she repeatedly sticks your arm to collect a greater volume of blood. There is now a good probability that the serum will have become hemolyzed as a result of its rough handling. The next thing you know is that the results come back showing very abnormal liver function tests. Although the physician is likely to rerun the tests, there is a good chance that somewhere in cyberspace there will be a report showing abnormal liver functions. Perhaps you may even be labeled a chronic alcoholic by someone who receives and misinterprets the erroneous information.

More and more U.S. executives, public figures, and others vulnerable to damage from medical information leaks are now taking their medical treatment needs offshore.

Exceptional medical facilities are available throughout Western Europe and Japan for major surgical procedures, cancer and AIDS treatment, cardiac care, and other serious conditions. Treatments for more routine ailments, such as hypertension, diabetes, back pain, drug addiction, and impotence, are available in an even wider array of places. Making the decision to seek medical treatment overseas to maintain your privacy does not necessarily mean sacrificing the best available care. On the contrary, physicians in Europe and Japan are not constrained by such agencies as the U.S. Food and Drug Administration (FDA) in offering the latest treatments and pharmaceutical products. The FDA is notorious for dragging its feet, sometimes for decades, in approving new medical procedures and medications even in the face of epidemics.

You must be prepared to sacrifice insurance reimbursement if you choose to take your medical problems offshore. Some variation of universal or nationalized health care is available to legal residents of virtually every nation throughout the industrialized world, the United States being the singular exception. Naturally you will not be eligible for this kind of free or deeply subsided care if the sole purpose of your visit is to get medical attention. Many private physicians and hospitals, however, will accommodate you on a pay-for-service basis. Fees in Western Europe for foreigners seeking treatment are typically 40 to 60 percent lower than in the United States for comparable services, so the financial burden will be lessened. Most important, there will be no sharing of Social Security numbers, diagnoses, or medical records with others. You will be able to return home knowing that your health records will not be disseminated to those who have no right to them.

SAFE DEPOSIT BOXES

If you do business offshore, you should also consider the vulnerability of safe deposit boxes you maintain for the storage of negotiable certificates, foreign currency, precious met-

Offshore Privacy: Issues Beyond Banking

als, or certificates evidencing your ownership of bullion or financial records. A secure box may prevent losses from fire or common theft, but it may also open a can of worms in the event of your death or incapacity.

In general, U.S. safe deposit boxes are sealed upon the death of their holders. The bank may be forbidden by law to allow access to your spouse or beneficiaries until your executor makes appropriate arrangements. The federal government as well as your state government will hover like vultures over your box, hoping to find assets that they can tap for their own coffers. The IRS may even send an agent to observe the opening of the box. If your box contains assets that you were holding in trust for your children, there is a good probability that Uncle Sam will treat these assets as having been yours, subjecting them to estate taxes. Should IRS agents find evidence of offshore accounts that had not been reported, the government might attempt to seize them.

It is therefore essential that you make arrangements to store your valuables, particularly those relating to offshore accounts or business, in a more secure fashion—one that will permit those you desire to gain access to your valuables upon your death. A relatively simple solution can be found by forming a corporation whose sole purpose is to maintain a safe deposit box. This perfectly legal technique can be done literally in a matter of minutes, no attorney required. Several states, including Delaware and Nevada, are particularly friendly to corporations. There are services that can do this for you over the phone or Internet for about $100. Maintaining a corporation requires minimal effort, including holding an annual meeting of the directors. Of course, the legitimate corporation can have as few as one director, so this poses no problem as long as you declare and hold a meeting once each year.

Corporations that do business in other states are termed *foreign corporations* and are normally required to pay a small annual franchise fee to those states in which it conducts business. Holding a safe deposit box is not considered the conduct of business, eliminating this additional nuisance. Since the corporation is an artificial person under the law, the death of any of its shareholders will not affect the corporation's access to its safe deposit box. The corporation's board of directors merely authorizes certain people to have access to the box and provides a copy of the resolution to the bank. The corporation can, of course, change the names of those authorized to open the box by issuing new resolutions at any time. In effect, the corporation isolates you as an individual from the corporation you wholly own.

Keeping the IRS away is not the only reason to have a corporation hold your safe deposit box. It also keeps a personal creditor from being able to have the box frozen by a court for an inspection of the contents, which can easily happen during a lawsuit or other claim against you.

For information on a highly recommended service that can form a corporation for you in Delaware (or in any state), write to the following address:

Inc. Plan USA
Attn: Incorporation Information Package
Trolley Square, Suite 26C
Wilmington, DE 19806
Telephone: 800-462-4633; fax 302-428-1274, marking the fax "Attn.: Incorporation Information Package"

Please note that Inc. Plan USA is only involved in forming U.S. corporations—it does not do offshore corporations.

KEEPING PRIVACY IN MIND IN DAILY LIFE

Moving your hard-earned money offshore is *legal*, but some governments and institutions want to make you feel as though it is not, so that you feel compelled to keep your money where it can be taxed. The situation sometimes borders on a witch-hunt. When it comes to personal affairs, nobody wants other people prying and looking into private information. Privacy is a right, not a privilege.

With more and more common working individuals looking into the possibilities of some form of offshore involvement, authorities of high-tax countries are getting more and more worried, and their policies are becoming harsher toward individuals who choose to free themselves from the burden of excessive taxing. When you have offshore affairs, it is best to avoid leaving a paper trail that is easy to follow, just to be on the safe side. Common sense and caution will help to accomplish this.

These are some of the favorite places where investigators look:

- *Credit card records*. One of the most revealing pieces of information investigators have. They reveal your movements, your interests, and your business relationships.
- *Telephone calls*. This includes both the ones you make and receive from and to hard lines and cellular phones, as well as fax numbers.
- *Banking transactions of more than $3,000*. By law they have to be reported to the authorities.
- *Garbage*. Believe it or not, there is a lot of information about individuals or families in their garbage. If you must dispose of statements, legal documents, or similar things, it is better to shred or burn them.
- *Mail*. The return addresses on your correspondence as well as packages you receive tell a lot about you. Customs officials routinely check correspondence.

I am just giving you pointers here; no need to become paranoid. Just use your common sense and don't leave too many flags about your movements, likes or dislikes, business relationships, or any other such thing. These precautionary measures should be observed not only in regard to offshore affairs, but life in general.

Chapter 9

The Swiss Connection

When they think of offshore havens, most Americans think of Switzerland, especially when they factor privacy into the investment equation. The Swiss franc has maintained stability better than any other currency. Unlike the U.S. dollar, which is backed only by the "full faith and credit of the United States," every Swiss franc is backed by a substantial amount of gold reserves. Switzerland has maintained its neutrality through two world wars and numerous other regional conflicts. It has therefore not suffered the economic consequences that other nations have sustained. In many respects, the Swiss enjoy democratic traditions that far surpass those in the United States: in Switzerland a national referendum process ensures that Swiss citizens directly determine all local and much national policy.

Traditional Swiss bank accounts are popular for all these reasons and more. Interest rates are modest at best, and earnings by foreigners have long been subject to a 35 percent withholding tax. Why then, one might ask, would U.S. investors deposit hundreds of millions of dollars in Swiss banks? One reason is that the Swiss franc has markedly appreciated against the U.S. dollar over the long term, partly offsetting the cost of withholding taxes. Fiscal and monetary responsibility by governments apparently pays dividends.

SWISS LAW AND BANK SECRECY

A second and perhaps more important attraction for American investors is that Swiss law protects financial privacy. For many centuries, Switzerland maintained an environment in which its people could bank in complete security, out of sight of others' prying eyes or even those of government officials. Naturally, this attracted worldwide attention long ago, and huge sums of money began to flow into Swiss banks for safekeeping. It wasn't until 1934 and the rise of the Nazis in Germany, however, that the Swiss government actually legally codified the heritage of banking privacy. The immediate reason was to protect Germans who had sent money out of the country to Switzerland to protect it against impending disaster (the German government made it illegal for its nationals to maintain foreign bank accounts).

Under normal conditions, Swiss government and bank employees are forbidden to disclose any information about bank accounts. It is unlawful for them to even confirm the mere existence of an account in the name of a particular individual. Enforcement is vigorous, with hefty fines and prison sentences meted out to violators. Additionally, such disclosures can be prosecuted under article 28 of the Swiss civil code, allowing those harmed by disclosure to recover monetary damages from banks and their employees.

Of course, customers can ask their Swiss bankers to release information as, for instance, in the case of requests for credit references. The banks cannot otherwise release information, however, unless ordered to do so by Swiss courts. Those who ask their banks to disclose account information as a result of a foreign court order may be considered to be acting under duress, allowing the bank to refuse such requests.

All the same, it must be pointed out that the Swiss system is not without weaknesses. Bowing to pressure from other nations faced with tax enforcement problems, Swiss banking privacy has been eroded in recent years. As a result of international treaties signed by Switzerland, the United States, and other developed countries, account information can be released when deposited monies are in some way related to crimes committed in other countries (though the alleged crimes must also be criminal offenses in Switzerland).

These treaties have only muddied the water because tax evasion is considered a civil matter in Switzerland, not a criminal offense. Nonetheless, allegations of tax evasion by U.S. officials are often accompanied by real or fabricated allegations of other criminal activities such as drug dealing, organized crime, or money laundering. The latter, now considered a crime in Switzerland, has put a new face on Swiss banking laws.

Under Swiss law, assets are presumed to be controlled by criminal organizations when they result from the commission of crimes and are therefore subject to forfeiture under the criminal code. Such asset seizures require a Swiss court order of forfeiture, which can be appealed by the defendant or his bank. In any event, the appellant has to show that the assets in question were not linked to criminal activity or that the amount was disproportionate to the gain actually incurred. Under articles 58 and 59 of the Swiss criminal code, however, the assets or bank deposits may still be frozen by the government during the appeal process.

The Strasbourg Convention (ratified by Switzerland in 1992) imposed new rules on Switzerland and others, requiring domestic confiscation procedures. In addition, even though it is not a member of the United Nations, the UN Convention against Drug Trafficking (1988) has put additional pressure on

Switzerland in this regard. Moreover, such international treaties impose obligations on states to confiscate the proceeds of crimes requested by other states that have signed or abide by these treaties. Assets transferred to innocent third parties have also become the target of seizure, although a number of exceptions have been stipulated to prevent severe hardships.

In 1996, the Swiss government allowed the Cantons of Zurich and Vaud to share more than $175 million frozen in 1994. The money had been deposited by a Colombian citizen in a couple of dozen accounts at a major Zurich bank. Swiss courts determined that the assets had resulted from criminal drug trafficking and accordingly seized them.

In 1995, Swiss authorities froze more than $100 million in deposits in a Geneva bank they believed were made by Raul Salinas de Gortari, brother of Mexico's former president, Carlos Salinas. Swiss police then arrested Salinas' wife and her brother when they tried to make withdrawals from the bank. (The accounts all bore fictitious names.) The U.S. Drug Enforcement Agency (DEA) had tipped off Swiss officials that the assets had allegedly resulted from money laundering and narcotics trafficking.

Coming to the aid of Salinas was one Carlos Peralta, a well-respected businessman heavily involved in the cellular phone industry. He insisted that he had given Salinas $50 million to invest in a capital venture fund and that as many as 20 other prominent Mexican businessmen had similarly funded the investment. The moral of the story is that guilty until proven innocent is no longer a strictly American philosophy. The DEA, IRS, and other U.S. institutions have extended their tentacles to the farthest reaches of the earth.

Drug trafficking and money laundering are not the only crimes that may lead to account disclosures or asset forfeitures. Switzerland has also made insider trading of stocks a criminal offense and has since cooperated with the United States and others in sharing information in this connection. In a recent case that eventually reached Switzerland's Federal

Tribunal (its supreme court), judges affirmed the right of France's Stock Exchange Commission to obtain assistance from Swiss authorities in such a case.

The litigation arose from a stock purchase in which a Geneva-based buyer acquired a block of stock in a French company just days before another group took control of a still larger stake. The French authorities found this highly suspect. The purchaser demanded that his name not be disclosed, arguing that the French Stock Exchange Commission had no powers to mete out penalties in France and thus could not proceed under the terms of any international treaty. But the decision of the court effectively broadened the powers of foreign administrative bodies to successfully collect information from their Swiss counterparts. Such information, however, cannot later be used as evidence in criminal prosecutions.

As a practical matter, then, Swiss financial institutions no longer offer the ultimate protection in financial privacy that once attracted millions of investors, savory and unsavory alike. Like the anonymous Swiss numbered bank account that is now a thing of the past, many earlier privacy protections have crumpled under the weight of international pressure.

By signing in 1995 the Hague Convention on the Service Abroad of Judicial and Extra Judicial Documents, as well as the Hague Convention on Taking of Evidence Abroad in Civil and Commercial Matters, Switzerland opened its doors to international mutual assistance in civil matters. To effect such assistance in criminal matters, the Swiss joined the treaties for Mutual Assistance; the Transfer of Sentenced Persons; and the Laundering, Search, Seizure, and Confiscation of the Proceeds from Crime. It has also entered into special bilateral agreements with the United States, Canada, Australia, Japan, and Russia.

The Swiss Federal Act on International Assistance in Criminal Matters puts some limitations on the role Swiss institutions can play in international requests for assistance. Courts will only compel the release of information when a crime punishable in both countries is under investigation. The information requested will be furnished only when direct relevance is established and then solely in proportion to the proof required. Even when information is furnished, it can be used only in connection with the agreed criminal proceedings. Foreign governments cannot use the same information to prosecute other administrative, fiscal, tax, political, or military matters.

Despite these trends, a referendum in 1984 affirmed by a very wide margin the Swiss people's desire to maintain bank secrecy. The Swiss Parliament specifically exempted tax evasion cases from judicial assistance in the international sphere, although tax fraud cases are still subject to information disclosure among treaty members.

Banking has been a major Swiss enterprise, and any further erosion in laws that protect privacy will surely cause money to pour out of its economy into more favorable repositories.

Switzerland still provides levels of bank secrecy and financial security that are uncommon in other nations, especially the United States. Those not involved in criminal activity can continue to benefit from Swiss banking practices; for the average person bank secrecy in Switzerland is more than sufficient.

Banks in Switzerland are tightly regulated by the Banking Commission and face comprehensive periodic audits. In addition, capital requirements far exceed those required in most countries of the world, including the United States. Historians know that the Crash of 1929 was largely brought about by massive runs on U.S. banks, with depositors lining up at their banks to close their accounts in the face of impending economic disaster. Of course, many U.S. banks had little or no liquidity and collapsed, leaving millions of depositors penniless.

It is true that we have a Federal Reserve system today that regulates capital and liquidity requirements. We also have the Federal Deposit Insurance Corporation (FDIC), which purportedly guarantees our deposits, at least up to $100,000 per depositor per bank. But many observers are skeptical that FDIC would be able to cover its obligations in the event of another national banking collapse. Recent events in both the banking and thrift communities suggest that a full-fledged banking system collapse in the United States may not be that far-fetched despite the reforms instituted since the Great Depression.

Additionally, Swiss accounting principles are more in tune with reality than those in the United States. Swiss banks are required to maintain 7 to 9 percent of their liabilities in hard equities. Securities they own must be valued monthly at cost or market value, whichever is less, preventing the accumulation of large portfolios of unrealized losses. Remember how Americans were stunned when savings and loan associations began to fold like paper fans? Their portfolios included billions of dollars in bad real estate investments, loans that had been effectively concealed from depositors and stockholders for years until collapse became imminent.

FULL-SERVICE BANKING: SAVINGS AND INVESTMENTS

One other unusual characteristic of Swiss banking is that it is broadly based. U.S. financial institutions and those of most other countries tend to specialize in one of two areas: banking or investment. The separation of the two functions in the United States was largely predicated on U.S. banking law that, until recently, precluded banks from selling such investment instruments as stocks, bonds, mutual funds, or real estate investment trusts. When this prohibition was lifted, Washington was plagued again with all sorts of problems. Many depositors, totally unaccustomed to investing at all, erroneously thought that mutual funds bought through U.S. banks were insured by the FDIC. Washington had to issue new disclosure requirements for banks dealing in such sales.

Some U.S. banks are now trying to do what the Swiss have done for generations. First Union, a giant in the U.S. banking business, began a media blitz in which it talked of two trains, one that served only the East Coast, and the other the West Coast. Its television spots show the tracks being joined, one train now providing both banking and investment services nationally.

Unfortunately, this trend in American banking may be too little, too late. U.S. banks have little experience on the investment side, and federal regulations still stymie the delivery of a full range of services. It is also important to note that Swiss banks have maintained branches for years in major financial capitals such as New York, London, and Tokyo.

More significant, however, is the continuing issue of privacy, something that simply cannot be provided by U.S. financial institutions on either the banking or investment sides. Privacy, coupled with an unsurpassed record of achievement in financial management, has drawn funds to Switzerland to the tune of two trillion dollars, half of the world's private portfolio business.

One of the leaders in Swiss financial management is JML Swiss Investment Counsellors, a firm that offers a unique style of financial management. Clients can customize and control their own portfolios and still receive comprehensive management advice from some of the world's best experts on financial matters.

Recognizing that investors have differing goals, time frames, and tolerance for risk, JML's managers work with individual clients to help them target their unique objectives. This naturally requires continued surveillance and analysis of worldwide economic trends, political events, financial markets, currencies, and other factors that could make some investments particularly attractive and others most unfavorable. Few individuals have the time or expertise to undertake this kind of evaluation themselves.

In any event, JML clumps the various opportunities that are available to investors into five separate categories for consideration by its Personal Portfolio Management Program clients:

- *Cash equivalents.* Principal and interest guaranteed for finite terms are provided.
- *Blue chips.* The investment portfolio consists of high-quality securities purchased for long-term capital appreciation potential.

- *Trading*. The portfolio consists of securities bought and sold for short-term capital appreciation.
- *Trends*. Often referred to a cyclical portfolios, securities are selected on the basis of economic forecasts by industry, sector, or country. The investor normally needs to wait about six years to realize significant annual returns.
- *Visions*. The most speculative of the five categories, investments are selected from opportunities in emerging markets and new technologies. It may take 10 or more years to realize larger annual yields.

For more information on JML write to:

JML Jurg M. Lattmann AG
Swiss Investment Counsellors
Germaniastrasse 55, Dept. 212
CH-8033 Zurich, Switzerland
Telephone: +41 1 368 8233; fax: +41 1 368 8299;
marking the fax "Attn.: Dept. 212"

(From most parts of the United States you need to dial 011 before the phone numbers.)

Potential U.S. investors may also want to consider the expertise of Weber Hartmann Vrijhof & Partners, an independent portfolio management firm. The principals of this partnership, former bankers and portfolio managers, provide services to individuals, offshore trusts, and corporations in need of investment advice. The minimum opening portfolio to be managed by this firm is $250,000 or the equivalent. The management team here normally recommends that a portion of the portfolio be invested in hard currencies other than the U.S. dollar, for example, the Swiss franc, French franc, German mark, and Dutch guilder. Respected for their conservative approach to portfolio management, the partners assist clients with opening a custodial account at one of the major private

Swiss banks, so that all client securities are held by the bank, not the investment manager.

A large percentage of their clients are based in the United States. One of their main goals has always been to get a certain portion of their clients' wealth out of the U.S. dollar and into European hard currencies and then build a portfolio with a mix of bonds and shares.

For more information, you can write to the following:

Weber Hartmann Vrijhof & Partners Ltd.
Attn.: New Clients Department
Zurichstrasse 110B
CH-8134 Adilswil, Switzerland
Telephone: +41 1 709 1115; fax: +41 1 709 1113, marking the fax "Attention: New Clients Department."

(From most parts of the United States you need to dial 011 before the phone numbers.)

SWISS ANNUITIES

Of special interest to U.S. investors are Swiss annuities. They are not subject to the 35 percent Swiss withholding tax on earned interest that is otherwise applicable to foreigners. These annuities, offered by Swiss insurance companies, are heavily regulated by government authorities to ensure adequate funding.

Most importantly, the issuers are exempt from all reporting requirements, ensuring that the anonymity of annuitants is preserved.

No government agency, Swiss or foreign, will ever receive information that a policy has been issued, that payments have been received, that interest or dividends have been disbursed. The investor can choose to have his annuity payments paid annually, semiannually, or quarterly. The policies are denominated in Swiss francs, but distributions can be made in any other currency desired, including U.S. dollars. Historically, Swiss annuities have paid yields equivalent to those of savings accounts at banks. They are arguably every bit as safe.

In many respects, the Swiss annuity looks and feels more like a savings account than a U.S.-style deferred annuity. Management fees are small, usually less than half of 1 percent, and there is complete liquidity, unlike with U.S. counterparts, which often require penalties as high as 7 percent of principal in the early years. A penalty of 500 Swiss francs and loss of accrued interest applies to liquidated accounts, regardless of size, but only during the annuity's first year. After one year, all principal, interest, and dividends are immediately available for liquidation.

Swiss annuities, unlike many American annuity and mutual fund products, are sold on a no-load basis, devoid of either up-front or sales redemption charges. By contrast, many mutual funds managed by the largest U.S. issuers apply fees as high as 5 percent or more when purchased or sold. Swiss annuities typically earn about the same rate of interest as long-term government bonds representative of the currency in which these annuities are issued. The investor thus gains the higher yields more often associated with long-term instruments and still maintains excellent short-term liquidity. Interest and dividend income are guaranteed by the insurance companies.

The investor can choose a lump-sum distribution at maturity, in which case capital gains taxes are payable on the aggregate earnings. He can also roll the annuity over into an income annuity, deferring taxes until income is received at a later date, or he can extend the term of the annuity with its issuer, allowing him to continue deferring taxes until it is finally liquidated.

Another special feature of Swiss annuities is that they offer excellent protection against creditors. They cannot be attached by creditors if the purchaser has named his spouse or children as beneficiaries. An individual with substantial assets can therefore protect a portion of his portfolio against creditors by investing in Swiss annuities. Annuities are insurance policies under Swiss law and are immune from seizure by creditors. The only caveat is that the policy must have been purchased at least six months before bankruptcy proceedings or creditor collection procedures begin. This is designed to prevent individuals from fraudulently shielding monies against specific judgments.

Such annuities will not be seized by Swiss authorities even if ordered to do so by foreign courts. Policyholders can convert their revocable beneficiary annuities to irrevocable instruments in the case of bankruptcy. Under Swiss law, the beneficiaries then become the policyholders with full control over the annuities. The original annuitant no longer owns the policy or has control, and cannot legally demand liquidation of the policy or repatriation of funds. When the beneficiaries notify the insurance company that a bankruptcy has occurred, the insurance company will ignore all requests or demands of the original annuitant to liquidate the policies.

The astute investor can thus shield his assets from creditors with fully revocable beneficiary designations. The change to irrevocable beneficiary designations need only be made if calamity strikes during the term of the annuity.

The choice of annuity payout options, incidentally, is made with the same considerations you would make for a conventional annuity issued in the United States. Your current age, life expectancy, and financial condition of your beneficiaries will determine what options best suit your needs. Straight life annuities, for example, continue to pay you for as long as you live, but your dependents receive nothing upon your death.

Annuities written with refund or for a particular number of years guarantee that if you should die early your designated beneficiaries will receive the accumulated funds or alternatively a specific number of periodic payments. The amount of the payment made monthly, quarterly, or annually depends on the option you have chosen, astute actuaries having calculated the probable payout the insurance company will make under these differing scenarios.

Swiss annuities may not be legally advertised or sold in the United States, but they are lawfully available for purchase by U.S. residents. In fact, they offer a special advantage for U.S. citizens. Because it does not qualify as a foreign bank account (or securities account), the Swiss annuity is not subject to the normal reporting requirements of IRS Form 1040 or other Treasury Department forms used for reporting foreign bank accounts. Fund transfers by check or wire are also not reportable since they are not cash or cash equivalents as defined by government regulation.

Banking with Swiss Insurance Companies

Another interesting twist to Swiss law is a provision that allows Swiss insurance companies to offer foreign investors the opportunity to bank with them. Investors avail themselves of all the advantages of Swiss financial transactions, including high yields, safety, stability, and secrecy. The premium deposit account with an insurance company, however, does not qualify as a bank account under U.S. law. U.S. residents do not have to report the existence of such accounts under current law. The Swiss apply no withholding tax to these accounts, and there is typically no ceiling on how much you can deposit. Even more comforting is the fact that premium deposit accounts normally pay higher yields than comparable bank accounts.

By maintaining a premium deposit account with the insurance company that holds your annuity, automatic premium payments can be made in a timely fashion. The most cost-effective practice is to make annual premium payments, avoiding the sometimes hefty surcharges imposed by insurance companies for semiannual, quarterly, or monthly premium payments. By avoiding the use of a Swiss bank account whose existence must be reported to U.S. authorities, privacy and anonymity can be maintained.

Premium deposit accounts cannot be used for purchasing

gold, securities, or other investments. It is designed as an interest-bearing account strictly for the purpose of funding associated annuities. Nonetheless, such accounts provide a safe, private, and financially sound vehicle for savings.

One final benefit of dealing with Swiss insurance companies deserves mention, although some would argue that it may be far-fetched. The establishment of exchange controls by the United States is not out of the question in the foreseeable future. The government would not likely institute such controls unless it became desperate, but some observers believe that the growing national debt may one day lead to measures born of such desperation. If history were to repeat itself and the United States were to reimpose exchange controls, such controls would be accompanied by the forced repatriation of investments held overseas by Americans.

However, it is probable that annuities and other arrangements with foreign insurance companies would not be covered by such drastic legislation since these represent pending contracts that have not yet been fulfilled.

Further information about Swiss annuities can be obtained by writing the following:

JML Jurg M. Lattmann AG
Swiss Investment Counsellors
Germaniastrasse 55, Dept. 212
CH-8033 Zurich, Switzerland
Telephone: +41 1 368 8233; fax: +41 1 368 8299; marking the fax "Attn.: Dept. 212"

(From most parts of the United States you need to dial 011 before the phone numbers.)

In the late 1990s there were minor changes in U.S. law that eliminated the tax deferral on all foreign *fixed* annuities for Americans. The Swiss very quickly came up with variable annuities that are fully compliant with U.S. tax regulations.

There are even IRS rulings on file that permit a tax-free exchange of a U.S. annuity for a Swiss annuity, so you certainly won't be out on some new frontier with your investment.

Swiss Perspectives Newsletter

Upon request to the above address, JML will provide any reader of this book with a free subscription to *Swiss Perspective*, a monthly newsletter on global trends and investment strategies, as well as news on Switzerland. This is usually about 6 or 8 printed pages per issue, so a full postal address is required.

PUTTING YOUR SWISS ANNUITY INTO YOUR U.S. PENSION PLAN

U.S. law requires that assets in pension plans be physically held by a trustee in the United States. For two products—foreign currency certificates of deposit and Swiss annuities—a service is available that will let you place these products in your U.S. IRA or pension account.

Asset Strategies International (ASI) of Rockville, Maryland, using the services of a major trust company, can provide the required custody and accounting services. Michael Checkan and Glen Kirsch of ASI provide a service that handles all the year-end currency conversion accounting required by IRS rules, and the trust company compiles the annual reports to the IRS. Checkan and Kirsch have been in the foreign exchange business for a combined total of 50 years. They are both well known in the financial newsletter industry, and at one time or another have been recognized as a "recommended vendor" by many of the writers in the newsletter industry. Among the many writers and publications recommending them are Mark Skousen, Richard Band, Adrian Day, *International Living*, and *Taipan*. Adrian Day, editor of *Adrian Day's Global Analyst*, says, "I've frequently recommended Michael and Glen in the past; you can continue to have confidence in utilizing their services."

For further information write to

Asset Strategies International Inc.
700 Rockville Pike, , Suite 400A
Rockville, MD 20852
Telephone (toll free in the U.S.): 800-831-0007;
fax: 301-881-1936

Ask for information on the offshore retirement account service. If you send ASI a fax or letter mentioning this book, it will place you on the free subscription list for *Information Line*, the irregular (but usually monthly) print newsletter with articles by a variety of writers on foreign currencies, international markets, and precious metals investments.

Chapter 10

Offshore Storage of Precious Metals

Taking physical possession of large quantities of gold, silver, or platinum naturally involves considerable risk. An alternative is the Perth Mint Certificate Program (PMCP), and it is an excellent way to safeguard your wealth securely, discreetly, flexibly, and inexpensively.

When you buy precious metals in the PMCP, you get a certificate of ownership. The certificate represents a specific item—the bullion or coins you purchased. The document simply shows "ounce for ounce" what you own that the mint of Perth, Australia, is holding for you.

The PMCP is an extremely private way to own precious metals. The PMCP is not considered a monetary instrument, since it is not negotiable and does not provide a payment of a "sum certain" in dollars. Your assets and any related documents are stored offshore (in Perth). You retain the ownership certificates, which are transferable but non-negotiable.

In case of an economic catastrophe, you simply use the documents to request delivery from Perth to any number of major financial centers, such as Zurich, London, or Singapore.

Some countries have restrictions on gold ownership, but you may remove your assets from the Perth Mint whenever you wish. There are no import or export duties on precious metals in Australia. Coins purchased in the PMCP enjoy worldwide recognition—you can liquidate them in any major financial market (subject to import restrictions).

The program also allows you your choice of gold, silver, platinum, or palladium. No other certificate program offers all four metals. And you can sell all or part of your holdings and receive your proceeds in a variety of currencies: U.S. dollars, Australian dollars, Swiss francs, or other major foreign currencies.

The PMCP's products are of the highest quality and purity Australian seminumismatic coins. They come in various sizes, ranging from 1/20 ounce to 1 kilogram (gold, platinum, and silver are available in the 1kg size). The PMCP offers low premiums, low storage charges, and a $50 certificate charge (per transaction). The bigger the transaction, the bigger the savings. Of all the available precious metal buy-and-store programs, the PMCP offers the most inexpensive way to buy precious metals, privately, in a convenient form. Now there's an easy way to hold part of your portfolio in precious metals and get the benefits of global diversification.

For more information on the exclusive Perth Mint Certificate Program, contact:

Asset Strategies International, Inc.
1700 Rockville Pike, Suite 400A
Rockville MD 20852
Telephone (toll free in the U.S.): 800-831-0007
Fax: 301-881-1936

Chapter 11

Offshore Managed Commodities Accounts

An offshore managed commodities account is typical of the type of investment available to an offshore corporation or trust but not in the United States.

The Dunn & Hargitt International Group, founded in 1961, has specialized in research for developing portfolio management programs that have the potential for providing investors a high return on their capital by investing in a diversified portfolio trading in the commodity, currency, precious metals, and financial futures markets in the United States and throughout the world.

The Dunn & Hargitt Group offers investors the possibility of participating in several of its different pools by investing through programs offered by its affiliate, Winchester Life in Gibraltar, but that are actually managed by Dunn & Hargitt.

At the time of publication, Dunn &

Hargitt is offering three possible investment alternatives, including the Winchester Life umbrella account (which allows 100 percent of a client's money to be invested in a diversified futures portfolio), the Winchester Life 100-percent guaranteed investment account (in which Lloyds Bank acts as custodian trustee and U.S. government zero coupon treasury bonds are set aside to guarantee the client's capital), and the Winchester Life 150-percent guaranteed investment account (which is a similar program, but guarantees that the client will receive at least 150 percent of the value deposited with a maturity date at least 10 years in the future).

The average net return for the 150-percent guaranteed investment account over the past six years would have been 22 percent a year. The average net return on the 100-percent guaranteed investment account over the past six years would have been 27 percent a year. The average annual net return for the Winchester Life umbrella account over the past 12 years would have been 35 percent a year.

The minimum accounts accepted are $20,000 for the Winchester Life umbrella account and the Winchester Life 100-percent guaranteed account and $50,000 for the Winchester Life 150-percent guaranteed account.

Although commodities are a speculative form of investment, investors everywhere are diversifying part of their portfolios to take part in the considerable potential profit opportunities that are available in the commodity, currency, precious metals, and financial futures markets. The programs devised by the Dunn & Hargitt International Group will make profits if significant trends develop in either direction (i.e., up or down). This does not mean that short-term results are always profitable, but the Dunn & Hargitt proven trading systems can provide above average returns over the longer term. Its objective is to make a profit of between 20 and 40 percent per annum for its clients, and its computer trading systems are geared to this level of performance.

For more information, contact the following:

The Dunn & Hargitt International Group
Department S-697
P.O. Box 3186
Road Town, Tortola
British Virgin Islands

The structure of Dunn & Hargitt has been established so that no taxes are withheld from the client's investment on the international commodity, currency, precious metals, and financial futures markets. Because of this, it can only manage money for investors who are neither citizens nor residents of the United States, United Kingdom, or Belgium, and the firm will not mail its brochures to those countries.

The Dunn & Hargitt International Group offers complete confidentiality to all of its clients and will not reveal any information about a client or its accounts to any third parties.

Chapter 12

The $70,000—and More—
Offshore Loophole:
Tax Planning for Foreign Employment

*I*f you're a typical cash-poor American, you could increase your standard of living dramatically if you could avoid throwing away 40 percent or more of your income on taxes each year. Thousands of Americans are doing that right now, and many more can. It's one of the clearest provisions in the tax code. In 1989, a congressman who visited Americans living in Europe told them that if the average American knew about this tax loophole, Congress would have to repeal it. As you will learn in this chapter, the loophole actually is broader, and allows you to earn far more tax-free income than even most expatriates realize.

The loophole is known as the foreign-earned-income exclusion or the "$70,000 exclusion." It allows for U.S. citizens who live and work outside the U.S. to exclude from gross income up to $70,000 of foreign-earned income. In addition, an employer-provided housing allowance can be excluded from income. There are other tax breaks available: each member of a married couple working overseas, for example, can exclude a salary of up to $70,000. That's a total of $140,000, *plus* housing allowance.

Although referred to as the $70,000 loophole, Congress has started slightly increasing the figure each year, so it is important to check on the current exemption if the exact number matters in your planning.

It is important to note that this is not a deduction, credit, or deferral. *It is an outright exclusion of the income from gross income.*

Naturally, to get these benefits you have to meet certain requirements:

• You must establish a tax home in a foreign country.
• You must pass either the "foreign residence test" or the "physical presence test."
• You must have earned income.

In the rest of this section, we'll discuss these tests and give some tips on maximizing tax-free income.

HOME IS WHERE THE MONEY IS

In the IRS view of the world, your tax home is the location of your regular or principal place of business. That is, the tax home is where you work, not where you live.

Take a look at what happened recently to one taxpayer who did not check the rules carefully. He is a flight engineer who lives in the Bahamas, but all his flights originate from Kennedy Airport in New York. The tax court ruled, not surprisingly, that his tax home is in New York, not in the Bahamas. The flight engineer does not qualify for the $70,000 exclusion.

But the definition goes further for the foreign-earned-income exclusion. This is a trap that catches many Americans overseas who think they are earning tax-free income. If you work overseas and maintain a place of residence in the United

States, your tax home is not outside the United States. In other words, to qualify for the foreign-earned-income exclusion you have to establish both your principal place of business and your residence outside the United States.

This trap catches a number of construction and oil workers. These workers generally work on a construction site or oil platform for three to six months. They get a few weeks or months off. Many of them make the mistake of leaving their family and personal possessions at their U.S. home and visiting this home during their vacations. They can't use the offshore loophole because they never establish a tax home outside the United States. They maintained a place of residence in the United States. *You need to sell or rent your U.S. home and establish a primary residence outside the United States.*

After establishing your tax home, you must pass one of two additional tests.

COUNTING THE DAYS

The more straightforward test is the physical presence test. To pass the test, you must be outside of the United States for 330 days out of any 12 consecutive months. The days, of course, do not have to be consecutive. That sounds very simple, but there are a number of smaller rules that can complicate it. Few people begin their foreign assignments on January 1 and end them on December 31. Thus for most people, the first and last of the 12 months of their overseas stay will occupy two tax years. This requires prorating the income and the $70,000 exclusion for those tax years.

In addition, to count a day as one spent outside of the United States, you must be out of the United States for the entire day. There are exceptions for traveling days and days spent flying over the United States if the flight did not originate there. The IRS has a number of rules on counting days.

If you are going to travel back and forth between the United States and foreign countries and if you want to try to pass this test, you'll have to learn the rules and count days very carefully.

An Easier Way?

The subjective test, known as the foreign-residence test, is probably easier for most taxpayers to pass. You must establish yourself as a bona fide resident of a foreign country or countries for an uninterrupted period that includes an entire taxable year, and you must intend to stay there indefinitely. If you do not pass this test, you are considered by the IRS a transient, or sojourner, instead of a foreign resident and will not qualify as a foreign resident.

According to the tax law, your residence is a state of mind. It is where you intend to be domiciled indefinitely. To determine your state of mind, the IRS looks at the degree of your attachment to the country in question. A number of factors, none of them decisive or significantly more important than the others, are examined. The bottom line is that you establish yourself as a member of a foreign community. The factors include the following.

Sleeping Quarters

A transient is more likely to sleep in a hotel; a resident likely owns housing or signs at least a year-long lease.

Personal Belongings

The more you take to the foreign country, the more you seem to be establishing a foreign residence. Leaving most of your personal belongings in temporary storage in the United States indicates an intention to keep that country as your residence.

U.S. Property

Owning a U.S. residence that you leave vacant is a sign of an intention not to establish a foreign residence. But selling or renting your U.S. residence indicates an intention to establish a foreign residence.

Local Documents

It is helpful to obtain a foreign driver's license and foreign voter registration when possible. But maintaining your U.S. license and voter registration won't kill your chances.

Local Involvement

You should show involvement in local social and community activities to the same extent you were involved in such activities in the United States It is also helpful to let U.S. club memberships lapse while you are overseas or to join similar clubs overseas. If you want to keep U.S. memberships in clubs that are hard to rejoin, see if you can convert them to a nonresident membership for the duration. (You may save on dues as well.)

Foreign Taxes

Foreign countries tax on the basis of residence. If you claim exemption from local taxes because you are not resident in that country, the IRS will conclude that you are a U.S. resident and do not qualify for the foreign-earned-income exclusion under the foreign-residence test. Thus some people prefer to qualify under the physical presence test rather than under the foreign residence test. With the physical presence test, you might be able to claim that you are not a resident of the foreign country and thereby exempt from its taxes. At the same time you can claim exemption from U.S. taxes.

Bank Accounts

This factor does not seem to greatly affect residence status. But if your case seems to be borderline, it is a good idea to open at least a local checking account even if a U.S. account is maintained. Many U.S. expatriates maintain U.S. accounts because it is easier to have their U.S. employers deposit paychecks directly in the U.S. account.

Permanent Address

You will occasionally complete documents, such as

passport applications, that ask for a permanent address. It is best to list a foreign address or some address of convenience, such as a friend's or relative's, from which your mail can be forwarded.

Once your foreign residence is established, you must show that it is for an indefinite duration. If you have plans to return to the United States after a definite time has passed, you are not a foreign resident. In deciding whether or not the foreign residence is indefinite, the IRS generally looks at your employment contract. (Note that it is permissible to have a vague intention to return to the United States someday. But if you have in mind a definite limit to your foreign stay, you will have problems establishing that you are a foreign resident.)

Generally, if your employment contract lasts for one year or less, that is an indication that you have a definite intent to return to the United States after a short period. You will not be able to qualify as a foreign resident. But if the contract is indefinite, open-ended, renewable, or likely to lead to a new job, you probably can qualify as a foreign resident. Therefore, it is best to have a contract that does not pertain to a definite project. If there is no written contract, the IRS will examine the nature of the job, the employer's personnel manual, and any other facts that indicate the intentions of you and your employer.

After establishing the residence, you can make occasional trips to the United States for business or vacations without losing your foreign-residence status. Just be certain that the trips are temporary and that you do not disturb any of the factors that qualify you as a foreign resident.

WHICH INCOME TO EXCLUDE

Once you have qualified for the offshore loophole, you must identify the kind of income that qualifies. *Not all income qualifies for the exclusion—only foreign-earned income.*

Foreign-earned income is income paid for services you

have performed in a foreign country. This includes salaries, professional fees, tips, and similar compensation. Interest, dividends, and capital gains do not qualify.

Self-employed people must adhere to some additional rules. Professionals who do not make material use of capital in performing their services can qualify all of their net income for the loophole. But when both personal services and capital are used to generate income, no more than 30 percent of net profits are considered eligible for the exclusion. Note that for self-employed individuals and for partners, the *net income* is the amount applied toward the exclusion limit, not the gross income.

Other types of income that do *not* qualify for the loophole include the following: employer-provided meals and lodging on business premises, pension and annuity payments, income paid to employees of the U.S. government or its agencies, nonqualified deferred compensation, disallowed moving expense reimbursements, income received two years or more after you earn it. But some of these payments—such as employer-provided meals and lodging on the business premises—are tax free under regular U.S. tax rules and retain that status. This is one way you can earn *more* than $70,000 tax free.

The $70,000 limit on the offshore loophole applies to individual taxpayers. So if you are married, you and your spouse potentially can exclude up to $140,000 of foreign-earned income. But you cannot share each other's limit. For example, if one of you earns $80,000 and the other earns $30,000, you exclude only $100,000 on the return ($70,000 plus $30,000).

Don't Close the Loophole

Too many U.S. expatriates inadvertently close the offshore loophole. There is more than one way to do this.

One way is not to realize that the provision has its requirements that must be met. Many Americans assume that since they are living overseas, everything they do is free from U.S. tax. That's not so. You've seen some examples of that in this book already, and there are other regulations for taxpayers in different situations. Special situations include not being over-seas for the full year and receiving advance or deferred pay-ments of income, bonuses, and other special income items. It is well worth your while to discuss the matter with a tax attor-ney or accountant who understands the offshore loophole. Go over your situation and your plans in detail *before* leaving the United States. That way, you'll be sure to qualify for and make maximum use of this loophole.

Another way people close this loophole is by not filing tax returns. To get the exemption, *you must file* a tax return and claim the exemption on Form 2555. The IRS has had success in recent years contending that anyone who does not file the return loses the loophole, even if he meets all the require-ments. Be sure you file the return and properly claim the loop-hole. The loophole exempts your foreign-earned income from tax, but it does not exempt you from the filing requirement.

Recent tax laws, plus some heavy criticism from the General Accounting Office, have caused the IRS to increase its monitoring of U.S. citizens overseas. The IRS now reviews passport applications and renewals to ensure that you do not receive or renew a passport unless your tax returns are filed and paid up. The IRS is also looking for expatriate Americans and informing them of their tax obligations. It is estimated that about two-thirds of expatriate Americans are not filing any U.S. tax returns, and the IRS aims to change that. Be sure to file your tax returns.

Tax Credit Option

Instead of excluding income from taxes, you can take a deduction for foreign taxes paid on the income. But the for-eign tax credit can get complicated, and in almost all cases, you'll find that it makes more sense to exclude income than it does to take the credit. But if your foreign-earned income exceeds the $70,000 limit, look into taking the credit for taxes paid on the income that exceeds the exclusion amount.

Beware Those Other Taxes

The disappointing part of the $70,000 exclusion is that it applies only to federal income taxes. The Social Security tax might still apply to salaried employees, and the self-employment tax might still apply to self-employed individuals. The self-employed, for example, still figure their net self-employment income on Schedule C. The net income up to $70,000 still is excluded from gross income. But it also is used on Schedule SE to compute the self-employment tax. For salaried workers with U.S.-based employers, the employer is supposed to withhold Social Security taxes. Possible exemptions are discussed later in this chapter.

Expanding the Loophole—Exempt *More* Than $70,000

The $70,000 offshore loophole is generous, but savvy taxpayers know how to make it even more generous. In many situations, you can exclude or deduct foreign-housing costs. You have an option here. You can deduct your housing costs to the extent that they exceed a base amount. Or if your employer reimburses you for the excess, the reimbursement can be excluded from income.

To get the write-off or exclusion, you must meet the same tests as for the foreign-earned-income exclusion. That means either establishing a foreign residence or meeting the physical presence test as well as establishing a foreign tax home.

The all-important base housing amount is 16 percent of the salary of a federal government employee with the grade of GS-14, Level 1. You use the salary that was effective on January 1 of the year you became eligible for the housing loophole. If you are not eligible for the loophole for the entire year, the base amount must be prorated, just as the income exclusion is prorated in that situation.

When your employer pays or reimburses you for qualified housing expenses, you can exclude from income the amount of the employer's payments that exceed the base housing amount. The employer's payments that qualify can be made in any of the following forms: part of your salary; reimbursements for housing, the education of your dependents, or tax equalization, or employer-provided meals and lodging that are not excluded from income under the regular tax rules. Any of these kinds of expenditures also qualifies for the exclusion if it is made directly to a third party instead of to you.

If you and your employer agree that a part of the payments received is for housing, but you have no firm agreement on how much is for salary and how much is for housing, you still get to use the housing exclusion. The excludable amount is your actual housing costs minus the base housing amount.

The exclusion cannot exceed either your foreign-earned income or the employer-provided payments for housing expenses. In addition, the exclusion for housing expenses is applied before the foreign-earned-income exclusion. The effect of this is to make it harder to exclude housing expenses against nonearned income, such as dividends and interest.

Suppose you are self-employed or your employer does not provide payment or reimbursement for housing expenses. In this case, instead of excluding the amount from income, you can take a deduction for the excess housing expenses if you meet the same eligibility rules as for the exclusion. The deduction is computed the same way as the exclusion. You subtract the base amount from your total qualified housing expenses, and then you subtract any employer-provided payments for housing expenses. Whatever is left over is your deduction.

The deduction cannot be more than the difference between your foreign-earned income and the combination of the foreign-earned-income limitation ($70,000), and any exclusion you take for housing expenses. In other words, your foreign-earned income must be above the exclusion limit of $70,000 in order for you to take the deduction. If you cannot deduct the expenses, you might be able to deduct some of them in the following year if your foreign-earned income exceeds the limit. Consult your tax advisor to see if you qualify.

A Few Limits

The exclusion or deduction for housing expenses applies only to reasonable housing expenses. The IRS gives no clear-cut definition of reasonable. Most tax advisors say that if your foreign housing is of the same standard that you were used to in the United States, it should be considered reasonable.

The following types of expenses qualify for this loophole:

- Rent
- Fair rental value of employer-provided housing
- Utilities, except telephones
- Insurance on real and personal property
- Occupancy taxes that are not normally deductible under U.S. tax law
- Nonrefundable lease fees
- Rent for furniture and accessories
- Repairs
- Parking fees

The following types of expenses do *not* qualify for this loophole:

- Capital expenditures, such the costs of purchasing, constructing, or improving a home
- Purchase cost of furniture and accessories
- Domestic labor
- Mortgage principal payments
- Depreciation
- Interest and taxes that normally are deductible
- Deductible moving expenses
- Pay-television subscriptions

The Second Overseas Home Loophole

A few taxpayers are able to exclude or deduct the expenses of *two* homes outside the United States.

To do this, you must show that the location of your tax

home, or principal residence, is subject to adverse living conditions. That is, the living conditions must be "dangerous, unhealthful, or otherwise adverse." If the location of your tax home is in a state of war or civil insurrection, you are living in adverse conditions. A different kind of adverse condition is when the employer's business premises are a drilling rig, construction project, or similar operation. The taxpayer lives there, and it is not feasible for the taxpayer's family to reside there. In this case, a second overseas home can be established for the family, and the expenses qualify for the exclusion.

If you think you might qualify for one of these exclusions, consult a tax advisor. There have been numerous regulations, cases, and rulings in regard to these matters. The tax advisor should be able to make sure you meet the requirements for maximum tax benefits.

Like the foreign-earned-income exclusion, the allowance for housing expenses is determined separately for spouses.

The Social Security Offshore Loophole

Not many people know this, but the U.S. has agreements that exempt overseas workers from either the U.S. Social Security tax or that of the adopted nation.

Most developed countries have some form of social security tax. The problem for many U.S. expatriates in the past was that many foreign social security taxes are far broader and have far higher rates than does the U.S. Social Security tax. In some countries, it is equivalent to our income tax, with rates above 30 percent.

The agreements, known as totalization agreements, dictate that U.S. citizens who are temporarily working overseas are subject only to the U.S. Social Security tax and are exempt from the host country's tax. The United States has signed such agreements with 12 countries so far: Belgium, Canada, France, Germany, Italy, the Netherlands, Norway, Portugal, Spain, Sweden, Switzerland, and the United Kingdom. A much larger number of countries will exempt you from paying the local social security tax, without a treaty, provided you present proof both that your employment is temporary and that you are covered by U.S. Social Security.

To be exempt from the host country's tax, you must qualify as a "detached worker." A detached worker is one whose assignment in the host country is expected to last five years or less. The wording differs somewhat in each treaty, so be sure to have that checked out before accepting a foreign assignment. If you are not a detached worker, you are exempt from U.S. Social Security tax and are subject to the host country's tax. The treaties also work for self-employed individuals. Many U.S. employers who send their employees overseas do not even know about these treaties; this ignorance prevents employees from minimizing taxes on their foreign assignments.

To qualify for the exemption, you must obtain a certificate from the U.S. Social Security Administration *before* the foreign assignment. You can apply for a certificate and get other information about these agreements by contacting the Social Security Administration, Office of International Policy, P.O. Box 17741, Baltimore, MD 21235. Pamphlets about agreements with individual countries are available from the same address.

THE PUERTO RICO LOOPHOLE

Some U.S. citizens find tax benefits by establishing residence in Puerto Rico. Since Puerto Rico is a commonwealth of the United States and has a similar tax system, the United States exempts income earned in Puerto Rico if you establish a bona fide residence there.

A residence is established as in the case of the foreign-earned-income exclusion: You must establish a permanent attachment to Puerto Rico and demonstrate an intent to stay there indefinitely, but in addition Puerto Rico requires that the residence be for the entire calendar year in question.

If you qualify, under Section 933 of the tax code you can exclude from U.S. income tax all income derived from sources in Puerto Rico. (Note that this exemption is all Puerto Rican–source income, not just earned income.) But this exclusion will prevent you from taking otherwise allowable deductions on your U.S. income tax for the income earned in Puerto Rico. Also, interest paid by Puerto Rican branches of U.S. banks does not qualify as Puerto Rican income.

You should check out the Puerto Rican tax situation before trying to qualify for this provision. You will be subject to Puerto Rican taxes, and Puerto Rico is not a tax haven. You might in fact find the country a tax liability: its rates are now generally higher than in the United States.

The one particularly interesting exception, however, is that dividends paid from a Puerto Rican company that has a tax holiday (such as the 10-year exemption granted to new factories) are free of Puerto Rican tax. One U.S. couple owned a small manufacturing business in Puerto Rico. In the tenth year, they sold the business but not the corporation, and paid a liquidating dividend from the corporation. Just before the tenth year, they had established residence in Puerto Rico and maintained it for the entire calendar year in which the liquidating dividend was paid. Total exemption from tax on the final payout!

THE STATE AND LOCAL TAX LOOPHOLE

The U.S. government taxes all its citizens, wherever they live in the world. Most foreign countries tax only their residents or domiciliaries. If a British citizen moves to the Cayman Islands and establishes residence there, he is not subject to British taxes.

U.S. states tax the way foreign countries do—based on residence. Therefore, when you establish a residence outside the United States, you avoid its state and local income taxes. For residents of high-tax states, this is not a minor consideration. About one-third of some people's U.S. tax bill is made up of state and local taxes. Take this into account when deciding whether or not to take advantage of the offshore loophole. But states have a broader definition of residence. Some states require you to sever all contacts in order to cease residency.

THE FOREIGN TAX LOOPHOLE

U.S. taxes are only part of the picture. Unless you move to a no-tax haven, you must examine the tax code of the host country to determine your tax obligations there.

Again, most countries tax on the basis of residence or domicile. The rules vary from country to country, but usually someone who has established a place of abode in a country for more than six months is a resident or domiciliary. This often means that *you can be considered a resident of two countries at the same time and can be subject to taxes in both countries.* Or you can be considered a resident of no country.

Different degrees of residence are taxed differently. For example, the United Kingdom uses the terms "domiciled" and "ordinarily resident," along with "resident." Someone who is domiciled in the United Kingdom is taxed in the United Kingdom on all worldwide income. Someone who is ordinarily resident or resident, but not domiciled, might be taxed only on the income derived from U.K. sources. The rule is similar in Ireland and a lot of countries whose tax laws were derived from the United Kingdom.

We cannot survey the rules of all countries, though some are profiled in this report, but you should be aware of this potential problem and consider it before deciding to take advantage of the offshore loophole. You might find ways to eliminate taxes from both the United States and the foreign country in question, or you might find ways to drastically limit the overall tax bite.

Another consideration is the double-tax convention, or tax treaty. The United States has tax treaties with about two dozen major countries. The intent of the treaties is to ensure that individuals and businesses are not fully taxed by two countries on the same income. But in many cases, the treaty can offer an even more substantial advantage than reducing the total tax bill from what it would have been had only one country—in absence of a treaty—taxed the income. Your tax advisor should check any treaty before you make a decision about the offshore loophole. See the chapter on tax treaties for more detail.

THE HOME SALE LOOPHOLE

If you want to qualify as a foreign resident, selling or renting your home is recommended. But selling the home is not always required, and many expatriates retain their U.S. homes because they plan to return someday. Expatriates who sell their homes after returning, however, could have some problems.

Take a look at one IRS ruling: A taxpayer purchased a house in Washington, D.C., in 1969 and used it as a personal residence. He was transferred out of the United States in 1982 and had someone house-sit until he returned to the United States in 1986. He sold the house in 1987 and moved to New York City. He planned to exclude from gross income $125,000 of the gain on the sale because he was over age 55.

But there was a problem. The tax law requires that you own the home and use it as your principal residence for at least three out of the five years that immediately precede the sale. Since the taxpayer was out of the country for most of that period, the house did not qualify as the principal residence, and he could not exclude the gain (Letter Ruling 8825021).

He could have avoided the problem by staying in the D.C. home for at least another two years, or he could have deferred the gain by purchasing a new home in New York City. He chose to rent an apartment. He could have sold the home before leaving the country, deferred the gain by rolling the sale proceeds into a home in the foreign country, and then tried to qualify the gain on the sale of that home for the $125,000 exclusion when his foreign assignment ended. But he did not properly plan for his foreign assignment, and he lost the tax benefit.

A similar problem occurs when people sell their U.S. homes before taking an overseas assignment. To defer the gain, you normally need to buy a new home within two years. Civilians have four years if overseas and military members have four years stateside or overseas. This replacement period is suspended while military members are stationed outside the United States. Note, however, that the replacement period, plus any period of suspension, cannot last more than eight years after the sale of the home. So if you are gone more than four years and do not purchase a foreign residence, the gain is not deferred. You can defer the gain by purchasing a foreign residence, since there is no requirement that the replacement residence be in the United States.

Chapter 13

The Tax-Free International Adventure:
Some Examples and Ideas

s the world's governments continue to attack traditional tax haven structures of paper holding companies and offshore bank accounts, the best defense is to actually do the business and live the lifestyle. Most attacks on tax havens come down to substance versus form arguments, and the problems almost always seem to come from the people who value the form over the substance. So they use things like offshore corporations and offshore bank accounts while filing false statements, or relying on secrecy and hoping the accounts won't be discovered. Or else they create a trust with a lawyer paid a small fee to be the supposed settlor and think that a U.S. court will believe that somebody in Bermuda miraculously created a trust out of thin air and named them the beneficiary of millions of tax-free loot.

How much simpler to genuinely be an offshore entrepreneur or an investor living offshore (as opposed to an offshore investor) or simply an offshore retiree. It isn't necessary to do it all at once. Just think internationally and gradually build an international business and lifestyle, in which tax savings and increased privacy are simply fringe benefits rather than the driving motivation. Whatever you manufacture can be exported, so think about setting up some foreign sales companies. Or suppose you have a travel agency—use that to make some tourism investments abroad. Perhaps you are a school teacher rather than an entrepreneur? How about creating a vacation business leading bicycle tours of Europe? The possibilities are endless if you stop letting the borders of your own country be your blinders. If you are in the real estate business, think about some international opportunities. Why not build your next apartment building in the Cayman Islands instead of your home town? If you trade commodities or stocks, and spend your day in front of a computer screen, that computer screen can just as easily be in your home in the Bahamas instead of your home on Long Island.

Do you want to live in paradise . . . in a palatial home with a maid and a gardener and a beautiful ocean view—all while cutting your taxes by 95 percent?

The international entrepreneur scene obviously places higher demands on individual ingenuity. Foreign laws have to be considered. Foreign customs, insofar as these relate to business dealings, inevitably have to be taken into consideration. Certainly, foreign distrust or acceptance of Americans will become a factor in many negotiating sessions.

But the complexities can be mastered. The green fields overseas can deliver paper of the same color.

How? At least 10 different roads to the creation or protection of wealth in foreign climes can be noted. Each of them involves the completely legal process of avoiding U.S. taxes by operating in tax haven countries.

1. *Establishing holding companies and trusts.* In most cases the personal holding company or overseas-based trust has a

specific purpose: to hold foreign currency or currencies or foreign currency assets. That means the trust or holding company may be an adjunct to a basic entrepreneurial arrangement. But there are few types of investments that cannot be transferred to a trust for preservation. The trust may also provide a guarantee against unnecessary dissipation of resources.

2. *Accumulating dividends, interest, and capital while conducting banking or financial dealings.* Here, a company is usually created; unrestricted fund movement becomes possible because withholding taxes are not assessed. The same company can realize big gains in European currency dealings.

3. *Amassing unlimited insurance premiums and interest income— again through establishment of a tax haven company.* The company, of course, can re-insure, co-insure, and perform other insurance functions any place in the world. Entrepreneurs seeking their own captive insurance operations have found the tax haven company an attractive alternative.

4. *Setting up subsidiary manufacturing operations that can sell back or lease products to a stateside parent company.* The tax-free operations of the subsidiary may involve assumption of commissions, discounts, and management income on the foreign sales of the parent group or organization. Thus taxes on the foreign sales are minimized.

5. *Engaging in sales and international commodity trading.* The entrepreneur with the appropriate background can establish an export-trading company or commodity brokerage operation. Working out of a tax haven, the company serves as a conduit for international sales activity and financing. Trade discounts, commissions, and advertising allowances can be accumulated tax free. The parent operation in the United States can claim tax deductions by assuming administrative and sales expenses.

6. *Expanding corporate or company operations into international*

markets to achieve growth and to provide a hedge against swings of the domestic economic pendulum. The tax haven operation with these or related purposes can accumulate tax-free revenue. If the company is engaged in industrial activities that create local jobs, the host tax haven usually offers tax, statutory, and other incentives and guarantees.

7. *Engaging in international shipping and air transport operations for such purposes as transportation, hiring, leasing, bunkering, and others.* Again, the revenues from such operations can be accumulated tax free. Beyond that, many tax haven countries offer flag-of-convenience privileges. That means foreign shipowners can register under the tax haven flag and in this way escape home country restrictions and regulations. The latter apply to taxes, competitive ground rules, and labor requirements, among other things.

8. *Setting up a tax haven intermediary company to conduct worldwide sublicensing operations.* The operations can, as needed, extend into such areas as royalties, payments in connection with patents, copyrights, inventions, models, designs, and secret formulas or processes. Caution should be exercised in establishing this kind of operation so that tax-at-source requirements are considered and accounted for. Where double-taxation agreements exist, these would also be important.

9. *Establishing mutual funds, investment trusts, and similar enterprises.* Where such groups or companies exist, overseas investors can buy directly into securities in their respective countries. They escape domestic tax liabilities, of course.

10. *Providing consulting services through a company or individual qualified to render technical, managerial, engineering, architectural, scientific, industrial, commercial, or other aid.* Where such services are provided across international boundaries, the foreign service fees can be channeled through the tax haven company.

WHERE TO LOOK FOR WHAT

The tax haven approach makes possible so many different types of enterprise, and these can appear in so many different forms, that a full enumeration is impossible. The form that each effort finally takes depends on the legal situation in the host country, as do the formulas governing shareholding, capitalization, and so on. Equally important is the nationality of the person doing the overseas dealing. The structure of a tax haven operation established by a U.S. citizen would differ basically from an operation set up by a Japanese citizen.

For the entrepreneur interested in exploring tax haven possibilities, various alternatives lie open. The entrepreneur can plunge in, obtaining experience as he goes, or he can ascertain where local tax laws favor tax haven operations by contacting a tax haven consulting company. Such a firm can structure an entire proposal describing the best way to take the plunge, get your feet wet, conduct the operation—and accomplish your goals.

The entrepreneur would normally have such a proposal double-checked by his own attorney.

There are still other avenues to venturing in international arenas. One, for example, involves taking a partner in a foreign country.

TAX HAVEN COUNTRIES

Experts on international business and finance say the tax haven countries house more millionaires per square inch than Wall Street. These tax haven nations have deliberately courted the interest and favor of multinational companies and operations. They have, essentially, passed flexible legislation that permits whatever form of organization is required to conduct tax-free or almost tax-free operations.

Normally, the entrepreneur makes the choice of a tax haven on the basis of geographical convenience. But other factors should weigh in the balance:

- The haven's physical resources and legal situation
- The haven country's political stability
- The quality, in a potential host country, of the specific services required
- In some cases the availability and reliability of labor
- Existing personal and other relationships, including those with lawyers, partners, bankers, special contacts, and so on.

Just as important, of course, the entrepreneur has to know what he wants to do from the outset. He may research heavily before deciding that question. Immediately afterward, he may want to establish in his own mind how the profits are going to be distributed and to whom, if more than one person is involved. If he is a citizen of the United States, he will want to ascertain what his citizenship will require of him. He will find, for one thing, that he stands at a slight legal disadvantage vis-à-vis his foreign counterpart. The latter may become a nonresident for tax purposes if he simply moves to a tax haven and takes up residence there, but Americans are subject to worldwide tax regardless of where they live.

Kinds of Havens

Tax havens are classified according to type. There are at least five basic categories.

1. *Those that levy no income tax.* These countries include the Bahamas, Bermuda, the Cayman Islands, and the Turks and Caicos islands.
2. *Those that do not tax foreign-source income.* Countries or territories in this group include Hong Kong and Panama.
3. *Countries that, like those in category 2, do not tax the foreign-source income of companies that are owned by nonresidents.* The countries or geographic entities that fall into this category include Barbados, Guernsey, Jamaica, the Isle of Man, Jersey, Liberia, and Gibraltar.

4. *Those havens that make special concessions for holding companies.* In this group are Austria, Liechtenstein, Luxembourg, the Netherlands, the Netherlands Antilles, and Switzerland.

5. *Havens whose tax laws make them ideal for special uses and purposes.* These include Andorra, the British Virgin Islands, Cyprus, Nauru, and Macau.

Combining Tax Havens

The possibility that tax havens may be combined should never be discounted. In a typical case, a combination may make it possible to avoid withholding taxes on royalties.

How does this work? The tax haven company first sets up a Dutch subsidiary—for example. The company then licenses its patents to this subsidiary. In its turn, the latter sub-licenses to a U.S. manufacturer. The royalty payments go tax free to the Dutch company.

The Dutch company then avoids Dutch withholding tax on dividends by paying the tax haven company—the patent owner—a royalty equal to those that it received.

The Dutch company would not be taxed in the Netherlands because its expenses equal its income. The tax haven company has acquired a royalty tax free. That royalty would, under other circumstances, have been subject to a 30 percent U.S. withholding tax.

The entrepreneur or multinational company desiring to incorporate in a tax haven country or area does not necessarily have to locate a headquarters there. Administrative offices may remain in another country offering greater geographical convenience. A Bahamian corporation could have its offices in Belgium. The company would in this case be subject to taxation on its Belgian-source income. But at the same time it would be appropriately located to conduct business in Europe.

THE MUTUAL FUNDS

Tax haven utilization has produced a kind of euphoria among some company management personnel. The offshore mutual funds industry provides a long list of examples.

Typically, these companies were not subject to either British or U.S. requirements about the length of time securities had to be held to qualify for lower capital-gains tax rates. Nor were the companies taxed at all on their securities trades and deals. Thus they engaged all too easily in short-term profit-taking and speculation.

International mutual funds like Fund of Funds and Gramco could invest in high-tax countries. Unfortunately, many such firms suffered from poor management. They went under after their managements became involved in excessively speculative sales campaigns. The campaigns dried up liquid capital; but collapse occurred when the mutual funds invested in funds that guaranteed to redeem their own shares at prices based on inflated book values.

The funds stand as object lessons in how not to do business internationally.

GET THE OVERSEAS PICTURE

As in any other phase of entrepreneurship, preliminary research is to ensure that an overseas venture will not only stand on its feet but will make big dollars. The reasoning behind this is simple. Statistically, the United States has less than 10 percent of the world's population, which means that 90 percent of the world's population lives outside the water or land boundaries of the United States. That makes for a rather large market. The preliminary study that the experts see as essential will indicate where penetration of that market is possible—and with what kinds of products or money-making ideas.

What to Sell?

Your research may guide your intuition into the exact area where offshore dollars are lying around ready to be picked up. But initially it may be wiser to keep an open mind. Just running through international trade magazines and newsletters looking at the listings may spark ideas. Those listings may or may not be the be-all and end-all of making a start in international trade. But they include the names of hundreds of overseas firms that want to buy U.S.-made products, sell their own products to U.S. firms, or represent U.S. companies overseas.

Do international business from your home? Why not? The listings in the publications suggest at least four ways to go:

- Find overseas firms looking for U.S.-made products and bring them together with U.S. firms making the desired products. You take a 5 to 10 percent (or higher) commission on all completed deals.
- Find overseas sales reps for U.S. companies.
- Become the international sales contact for a U.S. manufacturer and take a commission on all completed deals.
- Locate U.S. buyers of imports and overseas sellers. Bring them together and again cut yourself in for a commission on the resulting transactions.

Has it been done? Of course. In one case, entrepreneur Mike Johnson started an overseas product search and licensing firm on a grubstake of $300. Mike had no special secret. He used books and his own stationery. Once he got going, he found that he had to travel.

In four years Mike achieved two fundamental ambitions. He made more than 30 trips overseas, and he made more than $1 million.

He sold anything; he brought overseas firms together with U.S. firms that manufactured almost anything; and he represented U.S. firms overseas in almost any kind of import-export deal.

The Nitty-Gritty

Whatever you decide to undertake in foreign markets, some nitty-gritty facts stare you in the face. For the exporter of finished products in particular, the facts loom large, demanding attention. The entrepreneur considering entry into foreign markets via manufacturing should look at least at three specifics of an overseas or across-boundary operation.

Cost

When a U.S. company wants to compete with foreign producers of similar or identical products, cost becomes a controlling factor. To compete successfully, overseas production may become essential. In a typical case, higher labor costs in the United States plus shipping expenses and import duties may raise the price of a U.S.-made product well above the competitive level.

The Need for Proximity to Customers

A variety of considerations may dictate a need to manufacture near the locus of the major market. Products may have to be designed or redesigned to meet rigid customer specifications, for example. When a foreign government is buying U.S.-made products, the entrepreneur may encounter resistance to the idea of importing products that might be obtained locally.

Convenience, of course, goes with proximity. Manufacturing close to the target market obviously offers both advantages.

Alternatives to Exporting

Few companies can afford simply to pick up stakes and start over in a foreign country. Nor do many want to build a manufacturing plant in the foreign country of choice without exploring other alternatives. Nearly everyone in business knows of electronics firms that attempted to launch assembly-line operations in the current offshore assembly haven—only to surrender in ignominious defeat a year or two later when quality control had clearly become an impossible dream.

There are three alternatives to straightforward overseas manufacturing in leased or wholly owned premises that have proven extremely useful.

Contract Manufacture

Contract manufacture involves production by a foreign firm of the U.S. firm's products to the U.S. company's specifications and under its label. Large firms have turned in numbers to contract manufacture because the technique makes it possible to gain a foothold in a foreign market while maintaining domestic market penetration. Entrepreneurs have also used the technique. Establishment of a wholly owned subsidiary and plant may follow after a period of several successful years of overseas production.

Licensing

Licensing presents large-caliber complexities, but, done properly, it a way to tap the potential of foreign markets without risking a direct investment.

Some words to the wise may save the entrepreneur contemplating an overseas licensing arrangement from a bundle of headaches. The licensing plan should be worked out in every detail over whatever period is required—and it can be considerable. Potential returns should be assessed carefully in advance to make sure they will make the venture worth the effort. Also remember the following:

- The licensee should be carefully selected and investigated. The first candidate that appears, whether reputable or not, may not be the right one.
- The licensing arrangement should be drafted in such a way as to make it possible for the U.S. firm to control the licensee's activities. What you don't control, you can't trust. The U.S. entrepreneur will thus want to make certain

that he ensures adherence to agreements on product quality, royalty payments, the market area, and the use of the brand name. Provision should also be made for protection of the U.S. parent firm's interests—by manufacturing one or more components in the United States; registering patents and trademarks in the foreign country (including protocols on new products and improvements in existing ones), or both of the above.

- If possible, the U.S. firm's management should obtain an equity position in the licensee from the beginning. Later, if and when the enterprise succeeds, obtaining agreement on such a maneuver may be difficult or impossible.

Joint Venture

A final method of penetrating a foreign market involves creation of a joint venture. In this type of operation the U.S. firm not only holds a major equity position but can generally take part in management decisions to which it would not even be privy under a licensing arrangement.

The participants in a joint venture should carefully study one another's methods and philosophy before even signing an agreement. Each participant should understand clearly the other's management approach. Understandings should be reached on such areas of common interest as potential market position, financial policies, growth, and product development.

When a foreign firm is privately owned, don't forget to investigate the attitudes of the owner's family. Its members may have, or think they have, a loud and powerful voice in the firm's activities.

Entrepreneurs slavering over foreign markets should also remember the incentives that many governments offer to attract investment from the United States or other countries. These governments may provide tax concessions. They sometimes make long-term loans at favorable rates. They have even been known to construct plants for foreign investors—and then to assist in recruiting employees.

128

THE ENDLESS OPPORTUNITIES

Let your imagination wander. Think of Club Med. Sun, sex, and sand.

Think franchise. You can list 100 kinds of fast foods, junk foods, superfoods, takeout foods, trick foods, fad foods, foolish foods. Is there one that isn't sold by someone holding a franchise? In Japan, is there one man holding an all-Japan franchise under which he controls the books on every hamburger sold under the Big Yellow M?

Why not you?

The bloom is off the franchise rose, you say. True. But franchising still provides a way to get into international as well as domestic business.

Think of a big way to do it. A Seven Wonders of the World Way.

Fact: With some consistency foreign stock markets have outpaced those of the United States. Some of the foreign markets have the NYSE eating Paris', Tokyo's, or Rome's dust. An idea?

Fact: The U.S. firm setting up a regional office in various countries bordering the Mediterranean can enjoy substantial tax savings on foreign-source income. Among the countries that offer such advantages are Greece, Jordan, Tunisia, Malta, and Cyprus.

Fact: China—the People's Republic of China—has been fingered as the big hope for many U.S. firms (and, undoubtedly, individuals) in the 21st century. That, of course, posits the need for continuing good relations with the Far Eastern colossus.

FINDER'S FEES—
THE EASIEST MONEY
YOU'LL EVER MAKE

All you need to start is a typewriter, business letterhead, and a telephone. It is not uncommon for a professional finder to earn more than $100,000 a year. One finder earned $75,000 per month for five years. He saw an item in a newsletter offering 10,000 barrels of crude oil per day for five years. Putting that seller together with a buyer at a small refinery, he earned a fee of only 25 cents per barrel, and collected his fee of $75,000 every month for five years.

How about trading less than $1 in postage and a couple of hours' easy work for $100. Not a big fee, but it was so easy another finder couldn't pass it up. Reading a "collector's" magazine, he came across an ad seeking some college memorabilia from a college near his home. He made some local telephone calls, located the items wanted, wrote a letter, and earned an easy $100.

A finder is nothing more than a "matchmaker" for a fee. The professional finder simply matches qualified buyers with qualified sellers for a fee. A finder is not a pre-seller, dealer, representative, or agent.

Jim Straw, a nationally known publisher and entrepreneur, who has been a professional finder for more than 30 years, has written the only course in being a professional finder. To get more information on *Finder's Fees—The Easiest Money You'll Ever Make,* write to *Finder's Fees*, Department 70197, P.O. Box 5385, Cleveland, TN 37320 and ask for information on the finder's fee course. Or check his Web site at http://www.moneyhaven.com/phlander/

If a product or service can be sold or bought, there is a potential finder's fee just waiting for a finder with the "know-how" to earn it. There are finder's fees to be earned in every small town or big city, in every state and country. All you need to do is match up the buyers and sellers, put them together, sit back and collect your fees. And you can start your own finder's fee business for less than it would cost you for a good meal at a fine restaurant. All you really need are a typewriter, business letterhead, and a telephone to get started.

CONSULTING—ANOTHER PORTABLE INTERNATIONAL OCCUPATION

The "downsizing" of the U.S. corporation, coupled with merger mania, is creating a fabulous number of consulting opportunities for the individual who is prepared for them. In one case, the corporate brass had just dismissed all the in-house talent to do the job they now need a consultant for, and didn't want to "lose face" by calling the former employees back in as consultants.

Many computer professionals are now working internationally as independent contractors, yet rarely do they think of themselves as international entrepreneurs or engage in the financial planning that would let them take real advantage of their situation.

TAX HAVENS AND TOURISM

Most offshore companies engaged in real business can defer any tax until the profits are repatriated to the investor's home country. These are generally companies actively engaged in the conduct of a local business. In the travel business, such a definition is especially easy to meet. A retailer, or group of retailers, could set up their own travel wholesale operation in a convenient tax haven, such as Bermuda, and run all their European business through it. The profits of the Bermuda firm would accumulate tax free and could be invested in other foreign operations.

In addition, a great many countries offer tax holidays of 5 to 20 years for new hotel construction, often including smaller hotels down to as few as 10 rooms. A travel company or group of companies could easily invest some of their foreign profits in such a venture, continuing to build for tax-free profits. Among countries offering such incentives for hotel construction are Morocco, Jamaica, Tunisia, the Dominican Republic, Panama, most of the British-associated islands of the Caribbean, the French West Indies, and many, many more. Such concessions usually include an exemption from customs duties on building materials and fixtures.

Most developed countries do tax the current income of certain types of corporations controlled by their residents, such as leasing companies, and other financial enterprises dealing with the parent company. But this concept of a controlled foreign corporation applies usually to passive or tax-haven-type corporations, not to active businesses. But even for a passive business, a joint venture with foreign partners on a 50-50 basis will allow the income to accumulate tax free, since the company is not controlled by a national of either country. If you are leasing aircraft, coaches, or whatever, consider a joint venture with your foreign partner whereby you set up a jointly owned company to receive some of the income. You will both profit from it and have a tax-free pool of funds to invest together in other ventures. Such profits will not be taxed in the country of either partner until they are repatriated, since they are not controlled by either country's citizen.

Cruise ship operators have long been able to use Panama and Liberia, but they are about the only segment of the travel industry that has shown any understanding of the advantages of tax havens.

Many businessmen looking for tax-haven opportunities would envy the daily opportunities open to the travel industry, and yet the travel industry rarely uses these opportunities—or even understands them. It is a proven fact that 100-percent tax-free dollars will grow a whole lot faster than 50-percent after-tax dollars.

TAX HAVENS FOR THE INTERNATIONAL TRADER

All the information about the travel industry also applies to the international trade business. The international trader has available to him the same tax deferments and holidays as travel professionals enjoy, as well as the benefits of doing a joint venture with foreign partners. However, as with most of those involved in the international travel business, few international traders take advantage of these incentives.

Setting Up Your Tax Haven-Based Trading Operation

ICS Trust (Asia) Limited is a Hong Kong company that assists international traders in setting up import-export management in Hong Kong, usually making the company entirely tax free.

The handover of the former British crown colony of Hong Kong to China is complete, and it is now called the Hong Kong Special Administrative Region, generally abbreviated to Hong Kong S.A.R., even on official documents.

As more than one local businessman has put it, "Now that the politicians and journalists are gone [from covering the handover], we can get down to *business*." This attitude is typical of Hong Kong, still a true capitalist center. In fact, many of the wealthy who left to obtain second citizenships in Canada, Australia, and elsewhere have now returned to continue building their fortunes.

The major advantage of Hong Kong is simply that it is a real business center, not just a tax haven. One of the consequences of that is the ability to add value to services that are provided in only skeleton form in other tax havens. The reinvoicing business is a prime example. Most tax haven jurisdictions host a number of trading companies that do nothing more than reinvoicing.

Offshore reinvoicing can be a very useful tool for exporters as well as importers, since it allows for the accumulation of tax-free profits in an offshore environment.

Through reinvoicing, an offshore corporation is established as an international intermediary between importers and their suppliers or between exporters and their customers. The offshore corporation can thus either (1) buy products, on behalf of the importer, at the negotiated price level and then sell, or reinvoice, these same products to the importer at a higher price, thereby accumulating profits offshore where there is no tax liability and significantly reducing profits in the country of destination where there is tax liability, or (2) buy products at discount prices from the exporter, thereby creating a very small profit in the exporting country with tax liability and sell, or reinvoice, these same products at market value prices to overseas buyers, thereby accumulating profits offshore where there is no tax liability.

To be profitable, offshore reinvoicing operations need to be situated in an environment where import-export transactions are either tax free or have low tax (in relation to the onshore portion of the operation).

Once the offshore company has been established, the management corporation needs to acquire the services of a post office box, a telex, a telephone, and a fax machine for its use. When all are in place, the management company can begin reinvoicing. Of course, an offshore service provider can arrange these services.

The merchandise can be sent directly to the exporter's client or the importer. The only functions performed in the offshore haven are the preparation and dispatch of the new invoice and the management of the funds in the way instructed by the client and complying with local regulations.

But one Hong Kong firm has now developed this traditional service into a "real" business mode, with an ability to arrange local trade financing. This is a healthy step away from traditional tax havenry into a true offshore *business* center.

ICS Trust Company Limited is part of the ICS International group of companies headquartered in Hong Kong. This highly successful group was started by Elizabeth L. Thomson, who describes herself as "a lawyer by profession (two law degrees, a member of four law societies internationally), an entrepreneur by choice!" She has helped innumerable people start new enterprises in many parts of the globe and is well known in Hong Kong for her work with women entrepreneurs.

With a staff of 40, ICS can handle every aspect of your

business—from deciding to incorporate to obtaining financing from the bank to managing your paperwork, including letters of credit, to investing your hard-earned profits. ICS is truly a "one-stop shop" for entrepreneurs.

ICS clients range from multinational companies, for which ICS runs direct-import programs worth millions of dollars, to individuals who seek tax shelters and estate planning on an international scale. As an entrepreneurial group, ICS attracts many entrepreneurs as clients—business people who have grown their businesses to a level of maturity and profits that requires expansion into Asia for many diverse reasons.

Instead of starting just a paper-thin traditional tax haven reinvoicing company, with ICS you can develop a real business in Hong Kong. With its extensive banking contacts, ICS professionals will "shop" for the best letter of credit facilities that Hong Kong's competitive banking scene can offer, likely better facilities than you can find at home. Depending on the client, ICS can often arrange letter of credit banking facilities for clients with either a low- or zero-margin deposit, usually required by the opening bank. By freeing your collateral and capital, ICS provides you with more purchasing power to increase sales and gain higher profits.

Most of these reinvoicing transactions are usually done so that they are tax free in Hong Kong. There is no withholding tax on dividends, so it is often possible to engage in international trade through a Hong Kong company and obtain dividends from that company tax free.

ICS will also work with international banks and factors in Hong Kong and overseas to arrange financing, secured primarily on the strength of purchase orders from your clients. Working with banks, factories, shipping companies, and freight forwarders, ICS will structure a transaction to increase the likelihood of obtaining flexible, low-cost facilities.

The goods do not need to go through Hong Kong to use a Hong Kong vehicle to pass title. Most of their clients ship from a third country direct to their own country.

Although the traditional Hong Kong focus is on firms that trade in goods, it is also possible to use these reinvoicing structures in cases where services are to be provided from overseas. For example, a firm may contract a study to a Hong King company, which then may subcontract out the work to a third party firm—and the profit is kept in Hong Kong, tax free.

If you import goods from Asia for sale to large retail chains, ICS can help you expand your credit facilities and increase your domestic sales by establishing and running a direct-import program for you. Combined with ICS' international trade finance capabilities, the direct-import program is a powerful tool for generating more profits.

The primary goal of the direct-import program is to maximize your profits by making your customers perceive that they are buying "direct." This is achieved through the following:

- Setting up a subsidiary company in Hong Kong
- Getting your buyers to open their letters of credit (L/C) or orders to this subsidiary
- Communicating with suppliers to ensure goods are to specification

A direct-import program works because of two powerful reasons:

- The trend in the retail industry is for buyers to "buy direct" from the Orient. Having a subsidiary in Hong Kong that receives orders or L/Cs greatly enhances this perception.
- Large retail chains often can obtain freight and insurance at significant savings because of their economies of scale. Selling FOB Asia can often result in a lower selling price for the importer but with the same profit.

ICS will set up and manage the subsidiary company for you and prepare financing proposals for presentation to local banks. When everything is complete, goods are shipped directly from the Asian factory to the customer. The fact that you are now seen as an Asian supplier (and not the middleman) is often an important factor that clinches the deal. The added prestige of a Hong Kong office makes the customer think it is buying "direct" and therefore receiving the lowest price.

To get started, you should contact ICS with as much detail as possible about your business and its trading activities. For further information, contact:

Mr. Kishore K. Sakhrani, Director
ICS Trust (Asia) Limited
8th Floor, Henley Building
5 Queens' Road, Central
Hong Kong
Telephone: +852-2854-4544; fax: +852-2543-5555

(From most parts of the United States you need to dial 011 before phone numbers.)

You will be well advised and well serviced in the hands of this fine company.

SELL AMERICAN—AND MAKE A FORTUNE DOING IT!

What would happen if, in your business, all you did was "buy" from yourself? You wouldn't make very much money, would you?

Think about it! That's exactly what this country would be doing if we *only* "buy American."

Every time we sell an American-made product in the international marketplace, those dollars come back into the U.S. economy, increasing profits, creating jobs, making America stronger. About 80 to 85 percent of U.S. businesses don't export, even though American products are in demand. Amway recently went into Mexico, expecting $3 to $4 million in sales the first year. Instead the company hit $15 million in sales the first year and $50 million the second year, and said that it had never seen such strong demand for U.S. products in any of the more than 20 countries Amway is now in.

Yet it seems that when someone thinks about getting into international trade, the emphasis is on importing instead of exporting. Actually, exporting is just as easy as importing, maybe even easier. Besides, as an importer, you have to buy things to sell here . . . that takes money. But, as an exporter, you are selling things overseas . . . which doesn't take much money at all.

As a matter of fact, you can actually start your own export business with a couple of hundred dollars. Your very first order could easily return your investment tenfold or more. There are thousands upon thousands of products you can start exporting tomorrow. Most of the books and courses on exporting offered today are theoretical, not practical. In reality, selling overseas is no more difficult than a company in New York selling and shipping a product to a buyer in California.

A most useful complete startup is a manual called *Sell American*, available for $104.95 postpaid from the following:

Phlander Company
Department 70197
P.O. Box 5385
Cleveland, TN 37320.
Web site at http://www.moneyhaven.com/phlander/

Once you finish reading *Sell American*, you can export U.S.-made products simply and easily and start earning your fortune in the international marketplace.

With the end of the Cold War, the unification of Europe, the breakup of the Soviet Union, and the establishment of free-trade agreements in the Americas, every entrepreneur should now recall the words of Thomas Jefferson: "A merchant, by his very nature, is a citizen of the world."

While the governments discuss the issues of world trade, it is up to us as merchants (entrepreneurs) to meet the challenge head-on with action instead of talk. As an American entrepreneur, you should make it your responsibility to "sell American."

Chapter 14

Some Tax Havens
to Consider

tax haven is a country, enclave, or jurisdiction that encourages investment through a variety of tax incentives. These incentives might be in the form of specific tax exemptions, low rates, or tax holidays. Through the strategic use of tax havens, it is possible to significantly reduce your tax exposure and, in some cases, eliminate tax consequences entirely. Although there are places that promote themselves as tax havens and that in fact are dubious investment schemes that benefit only the backers of the scheme, legitimate tax havens are found throughout the world. Investing in them is fully legal as are the tax savings derived from them.

Not only do many of the following tax havens offer many methods through which tax reduction can be achieved, many of them offer a superior lifestyle and vast business opportunities as well.

ANTIGUA AND BARBUDA

Antigua, Barbuda, and Redonda (a rocky uninhabited islet) make up an island country in the West Indies, east-southeast of Puerto Rico. Together, the islands have an area of about 170 square miles (440 square kilometers). The islands are mostly flat and low lying, though Boggy Peak on Antigua is slightly over 1,300 feet in elevation (about 400 meters). The islands lie in the tropical zone.

Around 66,000 people live on the islands, most descended from Africans, British, and Portuguese. English is the official language, and British influence is found just about everywhere. Although not as well known or glitzy as some of the islands of the Caribbean, Antigua and Barbuda offer a quality lifestyle.

Investment and Taxes

Tourism is the mainstay of the islands' economy, but transportation, communications, and various types of trade are also important. The infrastructure of the islands is solid. Of most interest to those seeking ways to reduce their tax burden is that the islands do not tax personal income.

Contacts

Antigua and Barbuda Department of Tourism and Trade
25 S.E. Second Avenue, Suite 300
Miami, FL 33131
Telephone: 305-381-6762; fax: 305-381-7908

Antigua and Barbuda Department of Tourism and Trade
610 Fifth Avenue, Suite 311
New York, NY 10020
Telephone: 212-541-4117; fax: 212-757-1607

Antigua and Barbuda Department of Tourism and Trade
60 Claire Avenue, E., Suite 304
Toronto, Ontario
Canada M4T 1N5
Telephone: 416-961-3085; fax: 416-961-7218

Antigua and Barbuda Department of Tourism and Trade
Long and Thames Streets
P.O. 363
Street John's
Antigua, W.I.
Telephone: 268-462-0480; fax: 268-462-2483

Antigua and Barbuda
Chief of Mission
3216 New Mexico Avenue, N.W.
Washington, D.C. 20016
Telephone: 202-362-5211, 5166, 5122; fax: 202-362-5225

ANGUILLA

Anguilla is a small, low-lying island positioned at the northern end of the Leeward Islands in the Caribbean Sea. A British dependency, the island enjoys internal self-government. Anguilla has a total area of about 60 square miles (150 square kilometers) and a tropical, semiarid climate.

The island possesses several miles of spectacular beaches and in recent years has emerged as an important, if not well-known, tourist destination. Many who have visited it describe the island as a place offering a relaxing, unhurried pace of life. Anguilla has only about 10,000 residents, most of whom are of African descent. English is the official language, and British influence is apparent. The island's infrastructure is maintained by the British and is of high quality.

Economy and Taxes

Tourism provides the bulk of Anguilla's economy, as well as much of the island government's revenues. Taxes placed on hotels, imports, the sale of land to foreigners, a lottery, and British aid provide enough to pay for the government's expenses. Consequently, Anguilla offers a variety of significant tax advantages:

- No income tax
- No corporate taxes
- No sales taxes
- No taxes on capital gains
- No value added tax
- No taxes on interest

Contacts

Anguilla Tourist Board
World Trade Center, Suite 250
San Francisco, CA 94111
Telephone: 415-398-3231; fax: 415-398-3669

Anguilla Tourist Board
P.O. Box 1388
The Valley
Anguilla
Telephone: 809-497-2759 or 800-553-4939; fax: 809-497-2710

BARBADOS

Barbados is in the Windward Islands of the Lesser Antilles. It is the most easterly of the islands in the Caribbean and has an area of about 165 square miles (430 square kilometers). The island lies within the tropical zone, but its temperatures are moderated by the northeast Trade Winds. The island's picturesque scenery, abundant sunshine, and friendly people make it a prime tourist site.

The resident population of Barbados is about 260,000, of which about 90 percent are descended from Africans. Whites and individuals of mixed ethnicity comprise the rest. Large numbers of tourists may be found on the island throughout the year. The people of Barbados enjoy a high standard of living, a literacy rate of 98 percent, and one of the best per capita income levels of the Caribbean. English is the official language of the island. The island's infrastructure is modern and of high quality.

Boredom is seldom an issue in Barbados. The island's beaches are known for their beauty, and water sports are enjoyed year round. The island possesses fine hotels, restaurants, and theater groups.

Economy and Taxes

An independent nation, Barbados remains a member of the British Commonwealth, enjoying the status and advantages close association with Britain bestows. Unlike many islands of the Caribbean, Barbados is quite stable. The island's stability and democratic traditions—inherited from Great Britain—have enabled it to focus on development of its economy. In recent years, Barbados has emerged as a major telecommunications and financial center in the Caribbean. In an ongoing effort to attract investment, the government of the island has passed legislation that offers important tax incentives. Although many of the incentives are designed for companies that wish to expand their operations to the island, individuals can also benefit from Barbados's tax laws.

An individual's tax status in Barbados depends directly on his compliance with the concepts of "resident" and "domiciled." Anyone who is resident and domiciled in Barbados is obligated to pay tax on his income earned throughout the world. This can result in a hefty tax bill. To qualify as an island resident, a person must be present in Barbados for more than 182 days in a tax year. If you are present in Barbados for more than 182 days, but you are not domiciled in Barbados, you are obligated to pay tax on income derived from Barbados and also on any income earned elsewhere that is remitted to the island. This, too, can be a sizable tax bill. Nonresidents (those who are present on the island for 182 days or less in a tax year) are obligated to pay tax only on income derived from Barbados. With the generous tax incentives provided by the island government, tax on such income is likely to be greatly reduced from what it would be in other jurisdictions.

Because of the government's desire to encourage investment, tax incentives are aimed at those individuals interested in establishing a presence in the business sector. Following is a summary of the incentives included in the island's tax laws.

Significant business incentives (noted in the International Business Companies Act 1991-24) are detailed in the island's tax legislation, including the following:

- A tax rate of 2.5 percent on profits
- Exemptions from all local taxes on dividends, interest, fees, royalties, management fees, and other incomes paid to nonresidents
- Exemptions from taxes and duties on machinery, raw materials, computer equipment, and other items and materials imported into Barbados for business purposes
- Exemptions from local taxes on transfers of assets or securities, except in cases of transfer of real property located in Barbados or for equipment used on the island
- Exemptions from exchange controls
- A guarantee of the above benefits for a period of 15 years

Special incentives are offered to companies that provide information services, including these:

- A tax rate of 2.5 percent on profits for those companies specializing in data entry and whose business concentrates on international markets
- Exemptions from import tariffs on equipment related for production

Incentives are offered to companies in the manufacturing and export sectors:

- An tax exemption on corporate profits for a period of up to 10 years (Note that upon expiration of the exemption, export industries may be entitled to a tax rate of 2.5 percent.)
- An exemption from import duties on equipment and raw materials

International service companies engaged in offshore operations in Barbados are offered a variety of incentives, including the following:

- A tax rate of 1 percent to 2.5 percent on the profits of investment companies
- A tax rate of 2.5 percent for international business companies
- A tax rate of 2.5 percent on the profits of companies whose operations focus on technology service
- A full tax exemption for companies defined as "captive insurance companies," as well as a full tax exemption for U.S. foreign-sales corporations

In addition to these various tax incentives, Barbados offers numerous other incentives. Specific businesses may benefit from the following:

- Cash grants for training of staff and workforce
- Full and unrestricted repatriation of capital, profits, and dividends
- Simplified customs procedures
- Subsidies for space in one of the island's industrial parks
- The possibility of accelerated allowance for depreciation
- Free assistance with the procedures for investment in the island, decreasing bureaucratic red tape

Contacts

Barbados Investment and Development Corporation
800 Second Avenue
New York, NY 10017
Telephone: 212-867-6420; fax: 212-682-5496

Barbados Investment and Development Corporation
5160 Yonge Street, Suite 1,800
North York, Ontario MN2 6L9
Telephone: 416-512-0700; fax: 416-512-6580

Barbados Investment and Development Corporation
Princess Alice Highway
Bridgetown, Barbados
West Indies
Telephone: 809-427-5350; fax: 809-426-7802

THE BAHAMAS

The Bahamas are an extensive island group, beginning some 50 miles (80 kilometers) from Florida's east coast and stretching to about 60 miles (96 kilometers) from Cuba. Of the several thousand small islets and cays, only 30 are inhabited, with Nassau being one of the best known. The island group covers over 100,000 square miles (260,000 square kilometers) of ocean, yet the total area of The Bahamas are only 5,400 squares miles (13,900 square kilometers). The islands enjoy a delightful climate throughout the year, with great amounts of sunshine and average high temperatures of near 80°F (27°C).

About 280,000 people live on the islands, but the population is always higher because of tourists. The Bahamas are truly one of the world's prime locations, offering a wonderful lifestyle in a tropical setting. Although The Bahamas enjoy self-government, they remain a part of the British Commonwealth and ties to the United Kingdom are strong. English is the principal language, and British influence is found throughout the islands. The lifestyle one can achieve in The Bahamas is one of the finest in the Caribbean.

Economy and Taxes

Tourism, banking and financial services, pharmaceuticals, and the production of rum are important components of the economy of the Bahamas, with tourism alone accounting for close to half of the islands' gross domestic product (GDP). It is noteworthy that the chief source of government revenue comes from import duties, licensing fees for business, stamp duties, and departure tax. It is also noteworthy that the government of The Bahamas has not entered into any tax treaties with other countries. In an attempt to encourage investment, The Bahamas also offer numerous tax benefits, including the following:

- No personal income tax
- No corporate income tax
- No tax on dividends
- No tax on capital gains
- No tax on interest
- No tax on interest
- No tax on royalties
- No sales tax
- No payroll tax
- No tax on gifts
- No death duty for real or personal estates, and no succession, estate, or inheritance taxes

Contacts

Bahamas Tourism Office
150 E. 52nd Street, 28 Floor North
New York, NY 10022
Telephone: 212-758-2777; fax: 212-753-6531

Bahamas Tourism Office
P.O. Box N 3701
Nassau
The Bahamas
Telephone: 242-322-7500; fax: 242-328-0945

BERMUDA

Bermuda, a group of a some 150 islands, is located in the North Atlantic Ocean, east of North Carolina. Only about 20 of the islands are inhabited, and, of these, Great Bermuda is the most populated and well known. When most people speak of Bermuda, they are actually talking about Great Bermuda. The Bermudan islands have an overall area of about 20 square miles (52 square kilometers) and lie mostly near or slightly above sea level. All of the islands enjoy a subtropical climate that is mild and relatively humid. The climate, known for its delightful sunshine, makes Bermuda a popular vacation site.

The islands have about 62,000 year-round residents, but there are always thousands of tourists present. A dependent territory of the United Kingdom, English is the predominate language, and British influence is found throughout the islands. Bermuda's health care, education, and infrastructure are all of high quality.

Bermuda is one of the most affluent and prosperous jurisdictions in the world. Its GDP per capita of $28,000 is among the world's highest, and the lifestyle it offers its residents and visitors is exceptional.

Economy and Taxes

Most people think of Bermuda as primarily a vacation destination, but the islands' economic foundation is far broader than just tourism. Bermuda is also recognized for its financial services, ship repair, and pharmaceuticals. The island government also provides numerous and generous tax advantages, including the following:

- No income tax
- No personal taxes
- No taxes on corporate profits
- No taxes on personal or corporate dividends
- No capital gains tax

- No withholding taxes
- No gift taxes
- No inheritance taxes

Companies may also benefit from tax incentives. International companies registered in Bermuda may apply for an exemption from taxes on profits or income until the year 2016 in the event that such taxes are ever implemented in Bermuda. Such companies may be fully owned by individuals who are not Bermudan.

The only drawbacks for some individuals to benefiting from Bermuda's tax incentives are the cost of settling in the islands and the difficulty of obtaining a residency permit. In most cases, a resident is required to buy property in the islands that has a value of at least $1 million. Given that Bermuda is as close to a true tropical paradise as one can get—and considering its history of stability, minimal government bureaucracy, and lack of exchange controls—the cost of residency might not be so high after all.

Contacts

Bermuda Department of Tourism
205 E. 42nd Street, 16th Floor
New York, NY 10017
Telephone: 212-818-9800 or 800-223-6106

Bermuda Department of Tourism
245 Peachtree Center Avenue, N.E., Suite 803
Atlanta, GA 30303
Telephone: 404-524-1541; fax: 404-586-9933

Bermuda Department of Tourism
1200 Bay Street, Suite 1004
Toronto, M5R 2A5
Canada
Telephone: 416-923-9600 or 800-387-1304 (inside Canada);
  fax: 416-923-4840

Bermuda Tourism Office
Global House
43 Church Street
Hamilton, HM 11
Bermuda
Telephone: 441-292-0023; fax: 441-292-7537

CAYMAN ISLANDS

The Cayman Islands, consisting of Grand Cayman, Little Cayman, and Cayman Brac, are located in the Caribbean Sea about halfway between Cuba and Honduras. The low-lying islands are small, with a total area of about 100 square miles (260 square kilometers). They possess a tropical marine climate with somewhat rainy summers and dryer winters.

About 38,000 people reside on the Cayman Islands, although tourists and vacationers visit throughout the year. Indeed with their marvelous beaches and high standard of living, the islands are a popular destination. As a dependency of Great Britain, the Cayman Islands retain close ties with the British, who have maintained a modern infrastructure over the years. English, of course, is the main language, and British influence and customs are found throughout the islands.

Economy and Taxes

The Cayman Islands offer their people one of the highest standards of living in the world. With close to one million visitors each year, tourism is a major part of the islands' economy. The islands are also known as one of the world's leading offshore financial centers. Numerous major banks and financial services companies are represented in the Cayman Islands. To encourage investment, the island government offers important tax incentives, including these:

- No income tax
- No other direct taxation of any kind

Contacts

Cayman Islands Department of Tourism
420 Lexington Avenue, Suite 2733
New York, NY 10170
Telephone: 212-682-5582; fax: 212-986-5123

Cayman Islands Department of Tourism
6100 Blue Lagoon Drive, Suite 150
Miami, FL 33126-2085
Telephone: 305-266-2300; fax: 305-267-2932

Cayman Islands Department of Tourism
3440 Wilshire Boulevard, Suite 1202
Los Angeles, CA 90010
Telephone: 213-738-1968; fax: 213-738-1829

Cayman Islands Department of Tourism
9525 W. Bryn Mawr, Suite 160
Rosemont, IL 60018
Telephone: 847-678-6446; fax: 847-678-6675

Department of Tourism
P.O. Box 67
George Town
Grand Cayman, BWI
Telephone: 345-949-0623; fax: 345-949-4053

DUBAI

Dubai is one of the seven, oil-rich states of the United Arab Emirates located along the southern coast of the Persian Gulf. The state is small, and its land is mostly barren. Like many of the lands of the Middle East, Dubai receives only a few inches of rainfall per year. Summers are hot, and winters are mild.

Slightly over a half-million people live in Dubai. Most are of Arab descent; however, foreigners who work for the state make up a substantial number. Foreign workers come from many countries, the most from Iran, Europe, and India. Although Arabic is the state's official language, English is widely spoken, and both Arabic and English are common in business. The standard of living in Dubai is excellent, due primarily to oil wealth. Recognizing the importance of foreign professionals and workers to its economy, the government of Dubai has made provisions to make their stay in the state comfortable and enjoyable.

Economy and Taxes

Dubai's high quality of life is a result of the oil industry. However, the state's leaders, aware that the oil beneath the desert sands is expected to last only another 30 years at present rates of consumption, have embarked on a program of economic diversification. With the establishment of the Jebel Ali Free Zone and a modern infrastructure, the state's leaders hope to turn Dubai into a regional center for industry and trade.

Along with creating a probusiness atmosphere, they have also provided for numerous incentives for businesses in the Jebel Ali Free Zone. The incentives are available to domestic companies as well as those owned entirely by foreigners. The incentives include the following:

- An exemption from corporate taxes for at least 15 years. This initial 15-year period may be renewed for an additional 15 years.

- An exemption of personal taxes for at least 15 years. This initial 15-year period is renewable for another 15 years.
- An exemption from import and export duties payable within the free zone.

In addition, companies established in the free zone enjoy no barriers or restrictions on imports, no foreign-exchange controls, and minimal bureaucracy. There are no restrictions of currency in the free zone.

Contacts

Dubai Department of Tourism and Marketing
8 Penn Center, 19th Floor
Philadelphia, PA 19103
Telephone: 215-751-9750; fax: 215-751-9551

Dubai Department of Tourism and Marketing
901 Wilshire Boulevard
Santa Monica, CA 90401
Telephone: 310-752-4488; fax: 310-752-4444

ECUADOR

Although not always associated with the premier tax havens around the world, Ecuador offers several tax incentives that for some individuals can result in major benefits. The smallest of the Andean countries, Ecuador is located in northwestern South America. The country, with an area of about 110,000 square miles (285,000 square kilometers), possesses varying terrain from coastal lowlands to great mountains and dense jungles. Cotopaxi, the nation's highest point at 19,347 feet (5,897 meters), is the world's tallest active volcano. Although Ecuador lies over the equator (hence its name), its different elevations ensure that its climate varies. Jungle lowlands are steamy and hot, while temperatures in the higher mountains are cooler. Ecuador is a land of wondrous natural beauty.

Ecuador's population of 11.5 million comprises mestizos, Indians, Hispanics, and Blacks. The country's official language is Spanish, but several Indian languages are also spoken, mostly in remote areas. While a superior quality of life can be had in the major cities, the standard of living falls as one moves into the countryside. The country's infrastructure, similarly, is most modern in the cities.

Economy and Taxes

Ecuador possesses significant reserves of oil, which play a growing role in the country's economy. Ecuador also has abundant mineral resources, but much of its mineral wealth is located in remote regions and is difficult to mine. Agriculture is another important sector of the economy, with bananas, coffee, rice, and sugar being major export products.

Ecuador is recognized for its low cost of living in contrast to North America and Western Europe. Housing, food, and services in Ecuador are extremely reasonable by Western standards.

159

In an effort to encourage foreign investment the Ecuadoran government treats foreign and domestic investors equally and also offers tax incentives, such as the following:

- There is no tax on income originating from foreign sources. This includes (but is not restricted to) income from interest, dividends, and pensions.
- No provincial taxes, county taxes, or municipal taxes in Ecuador.
- There are no taxes on inheritance, gifts, or donations, except in regard to assets located in Ecuador.
- Capital gains are taxed at a rate of 8 percent.
- For income derived from Ecuadorian sources, income tax rates are quite modest compared with the rates of other countries.

It should also be noted that all investors are permitted to participate in the Andean Common Market without any restrictions. In addition, both foreign and local investors have easy access to foreign exchange for the remission of profits and repatriation of their investments.

As in Panama and the British Virgin Islands, the dollar is now the only currency—there are no local banknotes.

Contacts

Consulate of Ecuador
800 Second Avenue, Suite 601
New York, NY 10017
Telephone: 212-808-0170 or 212-808-0171; fax: 212-808-0188

Consulate of Ecuador
B.I.V. Tower
1101 Brickell Avenue, Suite M-102
Miami, FL 33131
Telephone: 305-539-8214/15; fax: 305-539-8313

Consulate of Ecuador
500 N. Michigan Avenue, Suite 1510
Chicago, IL 60611
Telephone: 312-329-0266; fax: 312-329-0359

Consulate of Ecuador
Wilshire Boulevard, Suite 540
Los Angeles, CA 90211
Telephone: 323-658-6020; fax: 323-658-1934

Consulate of Ecuador
151 Bloor Street, W., Suite 470
Toronto, Ontario
Canada M5S 1S4
Telephone: 416-968-2077; fax: 416-968-3348

GUAM

The U.S. territory of Guam is southernmost of the Mariana Islands. Located about 6,000 miles west of Hawaii, 1,500 miles southeast of Tokyo, 1,500 miles east of Manila, and 2,100 miles east-southeast of Hong Kong, it occupies a prime position as a gateway to the Orient. The island government's commitment to economic diversification and growth through a variety of tax incentives makes it a fine potential site for investment as well.

Having an area of 209 square miles (540 square kilometers), Guam is the largest of the Marianas. The island possesses a tropical climate with pleasant average annual temperatures of about 80°F (27°C).

Some 130,000 people are residents of the island. About 20,000 of the population are U.S. military personnel and their dependents who are stationed on Guam, which is a major Pacific defense site. The rest of the population comprises mostly Micronesians. English and Chamorro, the traditional language of Micronesia, are the principal languages of the island, with English predominating in government, business, and education. The infrastructure, telecommunications, and standard of living on Guam are good, all benefiting from U.S. presence and support. Guam may lack the exciting, bustling atmosphere of some of the Caribbean islands, but it offers an enjoyable lifestyle and exceptional environment.

Economy and Taxes

Capitalizing on its strategic position for trade in the Pacific, Guam's economy has expanded and diversified in recent years. The following sectors offer excellent potential: agriculture, aquaculture, construction, financial services, manufacturing, wholesaling, and retailing. Shipping is important, too. Apra Harbor, Guam's commercial port, is the largest deep-water port between Hawaii and Asia. It is designed to handle commerce, and it is considered by many to be one of the most efficient seaports in the world.

In an effort to foster the island's economy, the government of Guam, through the Guam Economic Development Authority, offers tax incentives to qualified investors. The incentives are based on investment commitment and the potential for creating new jobs with the primary objective being to expand the island's economy. Although various companies can benefit from the incentives, they are designed primarily for companies whose operations focus on one or more of the following: manufacturing, insurance, high technology, agriculture, specialized medical facilities, and fishing. Qualified companies may be granted incentives, including the following:

- A 100-percent income tax rebate for up to 20 years
- A 100-percent abatement on real property for up to 10 years
- A 75-percent rebate on corporate dividends for up to five years
- An abatement on gross receipts tax on petroleum and alcoholic beverages made in Guam for up to 10 years
- For firms licensed to do business on Guam an exemption from U.S. federal income taxes (but a requirement to pay a territorial tax)
- Interest earned through the operation of an off-shore lender not treated as a Guam-source income

Contacts

Guam Economic Development Authority
ITC Building, Suite 511
590 S. Marine Drive
Tamuning, Guam 96911
Telephone: 671-647-4332/4141; fax: 671-649-4146

Department of Revenue and Taxation
Government of Guam
Building 13-1
Mariner Avenue
Tiyan
Barrigada, Guam 96913
Telephone: 671-475-5000; fax: 671-472-2643

GUATEMALA

Guatemala lies just south of Mexico and stretches across Central America, giving it access to both the Pacific and Atlantic Oceans. Much of the country's area of 42,000 square miles (108,800 square kilometers) comprises highlands and mountains. Although the country lies well within the tropics, it has numerous local climates based on elevation. Lowland areas are humid and hot; highlands and mountainous regions are dryer and cooler.

Of the country's 12 million people, most are either mestizos or descendants of the Indians. Spanish is the official language, with about 60 percent of the population speaking it; the remainder of the people speak any of several Indian languages and their dialects. An enjoyable standard of living is attainable in Guatemala City, the capital, but much of the country is poor and underdeveloped.

Economy and Taxes

Throughout Guatemala's history, its economy has been rather weak, but many consider that the country has the potential for growth. Tourism is growing, with visitors seeking the nation's beaches and overall ecological beauty. A pro-business environment has grown in recent years and a free-market climate is prevalent. Most important, there are no limitations on foreign investment or foreign ownership of businesses or corporations. Moreover, there are no restrictions on repatriation of capital.

In late 2000, Guatemala legalized the use of the U.S. dollar in parallel with the local currency, allowing dollars to be used for all payments and to keep accounts.

To support the growth of businesses, Guatemala has established free-trade zones that offer numerous tax benefits. Incentives vary according to the type of company and business sector, including these:

- For companies located in a free-trade zone and that are engaged in commercial activities
  — An exemption from taxes, duties, or import charges on commodities and components stored in the zone for use in commerce and trade
  — A five-year exemption of tax on income gained from commercial activities that take place within the zone
  — An exemption of value added tax on goods transferred inside and between free trade zones within Guatemala
- For companies operating in the free trade zone and that engage in service and manufacturing
  — A 12-year tax exemption on income gained from the manufacture or providing of services arising from operations in the zone
  — A tax exemption on the import of equipment, tools, machinery, containers, packaging, and raw materials needed by the company for its operations
  — An exemption of value-added tax on goods tranferred between free-trade zones in the country
- For companies involved in the tourist sector
  — An exemption from all duties and import taxes on all materials and equipment needed for the business that are not produced in Guatemala or another Central American country
  — An exemption from real estate taxes on new construction and the expansion and improvement of existing structures and facilities

The way income tax is calculated according to the Guatemalan tax code may also benefit some investors. Although income tax is based on gross income, there are many notable exclusions, including the following:

- Interest from bonds or titles of government
- Dividends
- Any benefits already taxed in another form for the same tax period

As a means of assisting individuals who are considering investing in Guatemala, the Guatemalan Development Foundations (FUNDESA) has created the Guatemala Business Center (GBC). The GBC is designed to make investment in the country practical and efficient. The staff of the GBC offers up-to-date information on the business environment of the country, recommends contact people, agencies, and professionals who can be of further aid and can even help with scheduling visits to the country.

Contacts

The Guatemala Business Center
1001 Howard Avenue
Plaza Tower, Suite 2504
New Orleans, LA 70113
Telephone: 504-558-3750 or 800-794-GUAT; fax: 504-558-3755

The Guatemala Business Center
7231 S.W. 63rd Avenue, Suite 101
South Miami, FL 33143
Telephone: 305-666-0066 or 800-741-6133; fax: 305-666-0570

The Guatemalan Development Foundation
Diagonal 6, 10-65 Zona 10
Centro Gerencial Las Margaritas, Torre I, Oficina 402
Guatemala
Central America
Telephone: 502-332-7952 through 56; fax: 502-332-7958

HONDURAS

Honduras is another Central American country that, like Guatemala, offers various tax incentives in an effort to encourage investment. Also like Guatemala, Honduras is relatively small, with an area of 43,277 square miles (112,090 square kilometers), and has varying topography and climates. Along the coasts the weather remains tropical throughout the year but becomes a bit cooler and dryer in the mountains, which in some places rise to about 9,000 feet (2,800 meters). Volcanoes and impressive valleys are found throughout the country.

Honduras has about 5.9 million people, of which close to 90 percent are mestizos with the rest made up of Indians, Blacks, and Europeans. Spanish is the country's official language, but English is common among the educated, particularly in Tegucigalpa, the capital. Indian languages are also spoken, though these are generally confined to remote regions. Even though Honduras is one of the poorer countries of Central America, a quality lifestyle can be enjoyed in the capital.

Economy and Taxes

Despite the government's efforts at building a probusiness environment and strong economy, Honduras still lags behind many of its neighbors in economic output. However, several factors promise future growth. The overall infrastructure is good, and the telecommunications industry is rapidly modernizing. Puerto Cortes is the only deep-water port in Central America and it is also one of the region's most modern. The country's financial system is expanding rapidly and includes several major banks, an international airport serves the capital, and Honduras produces enough electricity to export to its neighbors.

To encourage investment the government has developed several free-trade zones and export processing zones (EPZ). Companies operating in the Inhdelva Free-Trade Zone, for example, enjoy the following benefits:

- No federal income tax
- No state (provincial) income tax
- No corporate taxes
- No local taxes
- No sales taxes
- No duties charged on the import of equipment or machinery, parts, raw materials, and supplies necessary to a company's operations
- Full exemption from export duties, fees, and controls

In addition, companies operating in the zone enjoy currency conversion without restriction and may withdraw capital or profit without restriction. They also enjoy various programs that enable them to ship certain products duty free to North America.

Companies operating in an export-processing zone are also eligible for incentives, most notably an exemption from taxes for as long as the company remains in the zone.

Contacts

Consulate General of Honduras
80 Wall Street, Suite 915
New York, NY 10005
Telephone: 212-269-3611

Consulate General of Honduras
1707 N. Burling Street
Chicago, IL 60614
Telephone: 312-951-6382; fax: 312-951-6394

Miami Consulate of Honduras
300 Sevilla Avenue, Suite 201
Coral Gables, FL 33134
Telephone: 305-447-8927

Consulate General of Honduras
3450 Wilshire Boulevard, Suite 235
Los Angeles, CA 90010
Telephone: 305-383-9244

Economic Department, Embassy of Honduras
3007 Tilden Street, N.W.
P.O. Drawer 4M
Washington, D.C. 20008
Telephone: 202-966-7702; fax: 202-966-9751

General Directorate of Export and Investment Promotion
4to. Piso. Edificio Salame
Tegucigalpa, Honduras
Central America
Telephone: 504-37-1850; fax: 504-37-8138

Honduran–American Chamber of Commerce
Hotel Honduras Maya Ap. Postal 1838
Tegucigalpa, Honduras
Telephone: 504-32-7043; fax: 504-32-2031

Tegucigalpa Industrial Chamber of Commerce
P.O. Box 3444
Boulevard Centroamerica
Tegucigalpa, Honduras
Telephone: 504-32-6803; fax: 504-31-2049

HONG KONG

When Hong Kong, officially the Hong Kong Special Administrative Region (Hong Kong SAR), was reunited with China on July 1, 1997, many people were worried that Hong Kong's robust economy and probusiness climate would deteriorate. This has not been the case. Today most people living and working in Hong Kong believe that the city will continue to be a center for business and investment opportunities for many years.

Located in East Asia on the South China Sea, Hong Kong consists of a part of the mainland and several islands. Overall, the area of Hong Kong SAR is 403 square miles (1,045 square kilometers). Its climate is warm in summer, mild in fall and spring, and a bit cooler in winter, though there are few extremes in temperature. Spring and summer are somewhat wetter than fall and winter, but, on the whole, the region receives ample sunshine and pleasant weather.

Hong Kong's population is about 6.7 million, of which close to 90 percent are Chinese. The remaining 10 percent of its residents include people from around the world. Principal languages are Cantonese (Chinese) and English, which is often used in international business. Hong Kong's infrastructure and telecommunications are of high quality, and its standard of living is one of the highest in the world.

Economy and Taxes

Hong Kong's GDP of U.S.$27,500 ranks among the world's highest. Its free-market system is one of the most open in the world, and the investment opportunities it offers are some of the best that can be found anywhere.

Hong Kong is one of the few jurisdictions in the world that can be described as both a business and tax haven. In most tax havens, a variety of financial services are offered, but there is usually little opportunity to add value to the services. For example, trading companies do little more than reinvoicing in the typical tax haven. In Hong Kong, however, the idea of a tax haven has been expanded to include that of an offshore business center as well.

In addition to its probusiness climate, Hong Kong also offers major tax incentives to investors, including the following:

- Only income derived from Hong Kong is taxable.
- Companies are required to pay only a 16-percent corporate tax, which is among the lowest in the region.
- There is no value-added tax.
- There is no sales tax.
- There is no capital gains tax.
- There is no withholding tax on dividends and interest.
- There is a commissionary corporate tax of only 8 percent for offshore business of professional reinsurance firms authorized in Hong Kong.
- Generous tax deductions are available for research and development.
- A 100-percent write-off for new expenditures on plants and machinery specifically related to manufacturing, computer hardware, and software is available.
- An initial allowance of 20 percent on capital expenditures incurred in the construction of industrial buildings and other structures is available.

Contacts

Hong Kong Economic and Trade Office
115 E. 54th Street
New York, NY 10022
Telephone: 212-752-3320; fax: 212-752-3395

Hong Kong Economic and Trade Office
1520 18th Street, N.W.
Washington, D.C. 20036
Telephone: 202-331-8947; fax: 202-331-8958

Hong Kong Economic and Trade Office
130 Montgomery Street
San Francisco, CA 94104
Telephone: 415-835-9300; fax: 415-421-0646

Hong Kong Economic and Trade Office
174 Street George Street
Toronto, Ontario M5R 2M7
Canada
Telephone: 416-924-5544; fax: 416-924-3599

REPUBLIC OF IRELAND

The Republic of Ireland should not be confused with Northern Ireland. Although the two share the island of Ireland, the republic is an independent nation while Northern Ireland remains a part of Great Britain. Because of the ongoing tensions between Protestants and Catholics, Northern Ireland garners much of the world's news headlines, overshadowing the republic that has quietly emerged as a haven for investment and tax incentives.

The Republic of Ireland covers the greater part of the island of Ireland, with an area of about 27,000 square miles (about 70,000 square kilometers). Northern Ireland has an area of about 5,500 square miles (about 14,000 square kilometers). The coast varies, being relatively flat in the east but characterized by islets and steep cliffs in the west. The climate of the island is about 25°F (14°C), warmer than one would expect to find at its northern position, because of the effects of the Gulf Stream. The island's average summer temperatures range between 57 and 68°F (about 14 to 20°C), with winter temperatures averaging between 40 and 45°F (about 7 to 14°C).

There are about 3.7 million people in the republic, with about one-third living in and around Dublin, the capital and largest city. Most of the population is of Celtic descent. An English minority is also present. English and Irish (Gaelic) are the country's official languages, with English the most common. The standard of living in the Republic of Ireland is comparable with most of the other countries in the European Union (EU), and the country's infrastructure and telecommunications systems are modern and advanced. The Republic of Ireland is a beautiful nation, considered by many to be one of the most pollution-free countries of Europe, if not the world.

Economy and Taxes

The government of the republic has taken various steps over the past several years to promote the country's economy.

Policies to promote the growth of light industry, tourism, and the financial sector have centered around substantial tax incentives, available to both residents and foreigners. The following facts demonstrate the overall strength of the republic's economy:

- The Republic of Ireland has only about 1 percent of the EU's population but attracts nearly 25 percent of U.S. investment in manufacturing in Europe.
- Over the past 20 years, 40 percent of inward investment in the electronics sector of Europe has been earmarked for Ireland.
- Of the 10 largest software companies in the world, five have development or production facilities in Ireland, which produces close to 60 percent of all the software sold in Europe.
- Of the world's top 15 pharmaceutical companies, 13 maintain research and development or production facilities on the island.
- The Dublin International Financial Services Center has emerged as the favored location in the EU for the financial services industry.

Truly impressive growth has occurred in the country's financial services sector over the past 10 to 15 years. Indeed, the republic has become a leading financial services center, with Dublin recognized as a major center for international offshore funds management in Europe. The nation's financial services sector includes various banks, investment and funds companies, credit companies, and credit unions. The many companies of this sector offer investors numerous services, including international banking, funds management, asset finance, and insurance.

A cursory look at the tax code of the Republic of Ireland reveals that although the country charges various taxes, including income tax, it provides major tax incentives as well.

- Foreign income (except income from the United Kingdom) is not taxable for nondomiciled residents, unless the income is remitted to Ireland.
- Nonresidents are not subject to withholding tax on interest payments they receive from a financial services company located at the Customs House Docks Area in Dublin.
- Manufacturing companies may be eligible for a 10-percent corporate tax rate. (The normal rate is 40 percent). For qualifying companies, the 10-percent rate is available until the year 2010.
- International financial services companies located in Dublin may be eligible for a 10 percent tax rate on profits derived from certified activities. In addition they may be eligible for a 10-year exemption on local property taxes, a 100-percent write-off for expenditures for new equipment during the first year of operation, a 100-percent write-off for the costs of new facilities in the first year for owners who occupy their sites, and a 54-percent write-off for new building costs in the first year for lessors. Companies may also be eligible to enjoy freedom of withholding tax in the payment of interest to recipients.
- Companies granted permission to conduct their operations in the Shannon Airport Customs Free Zone may be eligible for a tax rate of 10 percent through December 2005.

Contacts

Irish Industrial Development Authority, 17th Floor
345 Park Avenue
New York, NY 10154
Telephone: 212-750-4300; fax: 212-750-7357

Irish Industrial Development Authority
The Statler Building
20 Park Plaza, Suite 520
Boston, MA 02116
Telephone: 617-484-8225; fax: 617-338-4745

Irish Industrial Development Authority
P.O. Box 190129
Atlanta, GA 31119-0129
Telephone: 770-351-8474; fax: 770-351-8568

Irish Industrial Development Authority
75 E. Wacker Drive, Suite 600
Chicago, IL 60601-3708
Telephone: 312-236-0222; fax: 312-236-3407

Irish Industrial Development Authority
1620 26th Street, Suite 480 South
Santa Monica, CA 90404
Telephone: 310-829-0081; fax: 310-829-1586

Irish Industrial Development Authority
Wilton Park House
Wilton Place
Dublin 2
Ireland
Telephone: 00-353-0-1-603-4000; fax: 00-353-0-1-603-4040

Irish Tourist Board
345 Park Avenue
New York, NY 10154
Telephone: 212-418-0800 or 800-223-6470; fax: 212-371-9052
The Irish Tourist Board
Baggot Street Bridge
Dublin 8
Ireland
Telephone: +353-1-602-4000; fax: +353-1-602-4000

Irish Embassy in the United States
2234 Massachusetts Avenue, N.W.
Washington, D.C. 20008
Telephone: 202-462-3939 or 202-462-3940; fax: 202-232-5993

A Special Source of Help in Ireland

There is an Irish firm that I am particularly pleased to recommend. Fitzgerald & Associates, one of Ireland's leading accounting, financial, and tax consulting firms, is a dynamic, growing firm of registered auditors, business advisers, and accountants with offices in Cork and Dublin. The head of the firm, John Fitzgerald, is a law graduate and barrister as well as an accountant.

Apart from the usual accounting and auditing services, Fitzgerald & Associates is involved in comprehensive tax planning for both individuals and corporations, as well as in such corporate finance services as advice on funding, financial planning, management buyouts, and the negotiation of Irish government grant assistance. The firm gives advice on mergers and acquisitions and preparation of documents for public securities issues by Irish companies.

Fitzgerald & Associates forms Irish companies and can provide the company secretary and other statutorily required company services. To discuss specific services with a company representative, please contact

John Fitzgerald
Fitzgerald & Associates
6 Sullivan's Quay
Cork, Ireland
Telephone: +353 21 963877; fax: +353 21 310273

JORDAN

Surrounded by Syria, Iraq, Saudi Arabia, and Israel, Jordan is a Middle East nation with an enviable location as a crossroads. Through the Gulf of Aqaba in the south, Jordan also has access to the sea. With an area of approximately 35,500 square miles (90,650 square kilometers), Jordan is one of the smallest of the Middle Eastern countries. However, what it lacks in size it makes up with investment opportunities.

Jordan's climate is generally dry. Although the western part of the country has a rainy season that lasts from November to April (the wettest parts of the country receiving about 26 inches [66 centimeters] of rainfall annually), the eastern part of the nation has near-desert conditions. Temperatures similarly vary with location, with the Jordan River Valley experiencing extremely hot summer temperatures that may reach 120°F (49°C). Summer temperatures in other parts of the country often average 10 to 20 degrees lower than in the valley. Winters are cool, with temperatures in some regions occasionally falling below freezing, but there are seldom extended subfreezing periods.

Jordan has a population of about 4.4 million, of which some 98 percent are Arab. The country's official language is Arabic, but English is common among the country's professionals and upper classes. English is often the language of choice in Jordan's international business sector. The standard of living in the country is excellent, particularly in Amman, the capital, and the telecommunications system throughout the country is of high quality.

Economy and Taxes

In recent years the government of Jordan has undertaken steps to expand the country's economy, which for years has been based on agriculture and a few major industries. During the 1990s these steps resulted in impressive economic results, including some of the highest in the Middle East and North Africa.

During the past 20 years, Jordan has emerged as a regional business center, taking advantage of its prime location for trade and commerce. The government has also formulated legislation under the Investment Promotion Law of 1995, which provides for numerous incentives. Under the law, foreign investors enjoy the same rights and protections as Jordanian investors in most sectors of the economy, excepting construction contracting, trade services, and mining. The Investment Promotion Law divides the country into three regions—A, B, and C—according to economic indicators. Investors are eligible for specific incentives and exemptions in each region. The amount of tax exemption is determined by the location and type of project, including:

- Projects in Class A Development Regions, 25 percent.
- Projects in Class B Development Regions, 50 percent.
- Projects in Class C Development Regions, 7 percent.
- The projects in the above regions are also entitled to a tax holiday of 10 years.
- Projects planned at one of Amman's industrial areas are eligible to receive an extended "holiday" of two more years.

Contacts
Jordan Information Bureau
2319 Wyoming Avenue, N.W.
Washington, D.C. 20008
Telephone: 202-265-1606; fax: 202-667-0777

Embassy of Jordan
3504 International Drive, N.W.
Washington, D.C. 20008
Telephone: 202-966-2664; fax: 202-966-3110

Ministry of Industry and Trade
P.O. Box 2019
Amman, Jordan
Telephone: 962-6-663191; fax: 962-6-603721

Amman Chamber of Commerce
P.O. 287
Amman, Jordan
Telephone: 962-6-666151; fax: 962-6-666155

MADEIRA

Madeira, often referred to as the "Pearl of the Atlantic," is the largest island of a group of islands located near the Atlantic's prime shipping lanes, about 625 miles from Lisbon and 545 miles from Africa. Overall, the island group has an area of about 286 square miles (740 square kilometers). Although the islands are actually a part of Portugal, forming the district of Funchal, they are an autonomous region. The island government has taken advantage of this status over the years to draft legislation that has promoted the diversification of local industry and encouraged investment through a variety of tax incentives.

Madeira enjoys a mild Mediterranean climate with no extremes of temperature and precipitation. Add scenic beauty to its fine weather and it is easy to understand why tourism has become a prime sector of the island's economy. Indeed, several cruise ships make Madeira a regular stop so that their passengers can sample and enjoy the quality hotels, restaurants, and shops found throughout the island.

The residents of the island have descended from many people, with English and Portuguese predominating. Although Portuguese is the principal language of most of the population, English is also common, and both languages are used in business. Many of the residents are bilingual. The quality of life on Madeira is good, comparable with or better than the norms in Portugal. Excellent housing is available at reasonable prices, and visitors from the most advanced countries find in Madeira a modern infrastructure and telecommunications system.

Economy and Taxes

In hopes of expanding Madeira's economy and to improve the standard of living for their people, the Madeiran government in 1989 created the Madeira International Business Center (MIBC), whose purpose is to encourage and promote the region's business. The MIBC focuses on four major sectors:

- An offshore financial center, including banking, insurance, reinsurance, fund management, leasing, and other financial services
- An industrial free-trade zone, including all manufacturing and warehousing operations
- International services, which include various operations such as trading, holding, management, trusts, ship operations, and invoicing
- An international ship register, including commercial vessels, oil rig platforms, and pleasure yachts

In an effort to encourage investment, a variety of tax benefits are available to individuals and domestic and foreign companies.

- Specific incentives available to individuals include these:
  — An exemption from income and withholding taxes on dividends, interest on loans of shareholders, and other types of income received by investors in companies that operate from in the free zone
  — An exemption from transfer, gift, and inheritance taxes in respect of all transfers of shares in the capital of companies that conduct their business from within the free zone
- Incentives available to companies that operate in Madeira's free zone include the following:
  — An exemption from taxes on income derived from business activity conducted in the zone until 2011
  — An exemption from local taxes
  — An exemption from municipal property taxes in regard to income derived from business activity in the free zone
  — An exemption from transfer, gift, and inheritance taxes on the acquisition of real estate for the purpose of establishing operations in the free zone
  — An exemption from taxes on capital gains generated from the sales of fixed assets

- — An exemption from having to withhold taxes from the payment of royalties
- — An exemption from having to withhold taxes from interest on loans from foreign banks and on bonds issued by companies, provided these funds are used for investment solely in the free zone
- — An exemption from value-added tax (VAT) on imported goods, provided the goods are to be stored or transferred in the free zone
- — An exemption from custom duties on imported goods, provided the goods are to be stored or transferred in the free zone
- Specific incentives are available to offshore financial services companies, including these:
  - — An exemption from corporate taxes on all income obtained from operations conducted by the branch office, provided the operations are conducted wholly with nonresidents in Portuguese territory or with other individuals or entities established in the free zone
  - — An exemption from withholding taxes on revenues paid by branches in the funding of other business activities, provided the beneficiaries are nonresidents in Portuguese territories or are entities established in the free zone
- Specific incentives are available to service companies whose business activities include trading, trusts, and similar operations. The following incentives apply:
  - — An exemption from corporate taxes on income obtained from business activities until 2011, provided that such activities are conducted with entitles established in the MIBC or with nonresidents in Portuguese territory
  - — An exemption from corporate taxes on the interest of loans (The contracted entities must be established in the MIBC; also the loans must be used for operations in the MIBC and the lenders must be nonresidents in Portuguese territory.)

— An exemption for nonresident shareholders in Portuguese territory from corporate and individual taxes in regard to dividends and income from interest and other forms of loans and advances of capital until 2011 (The dividends must arise from the income of entities obtained from activities in the MIBC. This excludes the proportion of nonexempt income from business activities conducted in Portuguese territory.)
- Specific incentives are available to shipping companies through the International Shipping Registry of Madeira (MAR), including the following:
  — An exemption of tax on profits earned by companies that own ships under the Portuguese flag and transport cargo in international waters
  — An exemption from taxes on dividends that are distributed to shareholders
  — An exemption from duties on the inheritance of shares in a shipping company
  — An exemption from capital gains tax that would be otherwise payable on the sale or transfer of a ship or shares in a shipping company
  — An exemption from income tax on the salaries of the officers and crews of vessels operating in international waters

Contacts
SDM - Sociedade de Desenvolvimento da Madeira
Edificio SDM, Rua da Mouraria 9, 1st Floor
9000 Funchal
Madeira
Telephone: +351-291-201333; fax: +351-291-201399

Embassy of Portugal
2125 Kalorama Road, N.W.
Washington, D.C. 20008
Telephone: 202-328-8610 or 202-328-9025; fax: 202-462-3726

Consulate General of Portugal
630 Fifth Avenue, Suite 310-378
New York, NY 10111
Telephone: 212-246-4580 or 212-765-2980; fax: 212-459-0190

Consulate General of Portugal
3298 Washington Street
San Francisco, CA 94115
Telephone: 415-921-1443; fax: 415-346-1440

MALTA

Near the center of the Mediterranean Sea, located between Italy and North Africa, Malta has served as a crossroads between continents for centuries. Malta is the largest island of a group of islands that includes Gozo, Comino, Cominotto, and Filfla. Together, the islands have an area of about 122 square miles (316 square kilometers); the island of Malta has an area of about 95 square miles (246 square kilometers).

Malta enjoys a delightful climate with temperatures averaging about 89°F (32°C) in the summer and 57°F (15°C) in the winter. Sunshine is plentiful.

About 380,000 people whose ancestry represents many of the lands around the Mediterranean and Europe live on Malta, enjoying a diverse and multifaceted culture. English is the islands' official language, with Maltese and Italian also widely spoken. The standard of living on Malta is among the best of Europe, quality health care is available to just about everyone, education is valued and free on all levels, and the infrastructure of the islands is fully modern.

Economy and Taxes

Malta has a diversified economy built around various industries, including textiles, high-tech products, machinery, food and beverages, and tourism. In recent years, Malta has also grown in importance as an international financial services center. Numerous banks and financial services companies offer an astounding assortment of financial products and services.

With a goal of promoting investment in Malta and sustaining the islands' economy, the government has included various tax exemptions and incentives aimed at both individuals and companies. Following are incentives for individuals:

- There are no property taxes, real estate taxes, local, or municipal taxes in Malta.

- Income arising outside of Malta, including capital gains, is subject to tax only if the recipient is both domiciled in and a resident of Malta.
- Expatriates are not required to pay tax on capital gains.
- Foreign residents are taxed only a small percentage on the amount they bring into the country for living expenses.

The following incentives are designed for businesses:

- Companies that are at least 95 percent export oriented may receive a tax holiday of 10 years.
- Companies may be eligible for special investment tax credits.
- Specific companies may be eligible for an accelerated allowance for depreciation.
- Specific companies may be eligible for reduced rates for reinvested profits.
- Specific companies may be eligible for duty-free importation of parts or materials.
- Specific companies may be eligible for duty-free shipment of various products shipped to EU countries.
- Specific companies may be eligible for reduced tariffs on products exported to the United States.

Contacts

Malta National Tourist Office
Empire State Building
350 Fifth Avenue, Suite 4412
New York, NY 10118
Telephone: 212-695-9520; fax: 212-695-8229

Malta Tourist Office
280 Republic Street
Valletta CMR 02
Malta
Telephone: 22-44-44/5 or 22-50-48/9; fax: 22-04-01

Embassy of Malta
2017 Connecticut Avenue, N.W.
Washington, D.C. 20008
Telephone: 202-462-3611/2; fax: 202-387-5470

Malta Development Corporation
P.O. Box 141
Marsa GPO 01
Malta
Telephone: +356-667-100; fax: +356-667-111

COMMONWEALTH OF THE
NORTHERN MARIANA ISLANDS

Saipan, Tinia, and Rota are the principal islands of the Northern Marianas, an archipelago of numerous islands located in the western Pacific Ocean. (Guam is also a part of the archipelago, but it is not a member of the Commonwealth. See the section on Guam.) The overall land area of the Marianas is about 184 square miles (477 square kilometers). Saipan is the largest island, with Tinian and Rota next in area. Saipan, home to the islands' government, is a busy seaport and possesses an international airport. The Marianas enjoy a tropical climate with average annual temperatures of about 83°F (28°C) and little seasonal variation. Sunshine graces most days.

About 53,500 people live on the Marianas, with close to 90 percent residing on Saipan. The population is composed of various Pacific people, but also includes Americans, Koreans, Filipinos, Japanese, and Chinese. Several languages are spoken throughout the islands with English, Chamorro (a native language), and Carolinian being official languages. Along with the climate and natural beauty, the excellent standard of living in the Marianas, particularly Saipan, makes the Marianas a true Pacific paradise.

Economy and Taxes

In an effort to attract investment, the government of the Commonwealth of the Northern Mariana Islands has enacted legislation that provides significant incentives, including these:

- A rebate of up to 95 percent on taxes is paid on personal income, provided that such taxes as paid do not surpass $7.5 million. (Residency requirements must be satisfied.)
- A rebate of up to 95 percent on taxes is paid on corporate income, provided that such taxes as paid do not surpass $7.5 million. (Residency requirements must be satisfied.)
- Foreign companies are eligible for federal tax reductions on a

part of the income they generate from the sales of exports, provided they conduct their business from a location in the commonwealth. Moreover, these companies are not required to pay tax to the government of the commonwealth.
- All ports of entry are free of U.S. customs duties.
- Specific goods may be exported to the U.S. duty free and without quota restrictions.

Contacts

Office of the Governor
Administration Building
Capitol Hill
Saipan, MP 96950
Telephone: 670-322-5091-92; fax: 670-322-5096

Marianas Visitors' Authority
P.O. Box 861
Saipan, MP 96950
Telephone: 670-664-3200/1; fax: 670-664-3237

Saipan Division of Revenue and Taxation
Department of Finance
CNMI Government
Saipan, MP 96950
Telephone: 670-664-1000; fax: 670-664-1115

Saipan Chamber of Commerce
P.O. Box 806 CHRB
Saipan, MP 96950
Telephone: 670-233-7150; fax: 670-233-7151

Department of Commerce
Commonwealth of the Northern Mariana Islands
Caller Box 10007 CK
Saipan, MP 96950
Telephone: 670-664-3000; fax: 670-664-3066/67

MONACO

Located in southeastern France, Monaco is a small independent principality with an area of slightly less than a square mile. Best known as a resort of the rich, the enclave is in fact affordable for investors of modest means. Surrounded by France except on the south where the Mediterranean touches its shores, Monaco possesses a climate with few extremes. Mild winters and warm summers with plenty of sunshine through the year make the enclave a delightful place. Monaco is a wealthy enclave that offers its residents one of the finest lifestyles in the world.

Some 30,000 people reside in Monaco. About 12,000 of the enclave's residents are French, 5,000 are Italian, and 5,000 are Monegasques, with the remainder composed of other Europeans. Monaco's official language is French; however, many of the residents speak Monegasque, a mixture of French and Italian. English is also common.

Economy and Taxes

Several sectors provide the foundation of Monaco's economy, including tourism, banking and insurance, and the production of electronic equipment, pharmaceuticals, and cosmetics. The gambling casino at Monte Carlo also is a major source of government revenue. Some of the world's largest banks, including American Express, Citibank, Chase, Credit Suisse, Grindlays, and NatWest, are represented in Monaco. The government offers various tax incentives:

- Monaco has no personal income tax. French nationals under specific conditions are excluded, however.
- The Monegasque fund, a special fund created in Monaco, is not subject to income tax or capital gains tax in the enclave. Also, investors in the fund are not subject to income tax or capital gains tax from the fund's proceeds in Monaco.

- Closely held investment trusts enjoy locally tax-free administration.

Contacts

Monaco Government Tourist and Convention Bureau
565 Fifth Avenue
New York, NY 10017
Telephone: 212-286-3330 or 800-753-9696; fax: 212-286-9890

Monaco Tourist Board and Convention Bureau
2A, Boulevard des Moulins
Monte Carlo, MC 98000
Monaco
Telephone: 377-92-166116; fax: 377-92-166000

PANAMA

Positioned at the southernmost part of North America, Panama links the north with South America. The republic is also home to the Panama Canal, which it officially took control of from the United States at the end of 1999. A long, narrow country, highlighted with rugged interior mountains, Panama has an area of 29,762 square miles (77,082 square kilometers). It has easy access to both the Atlantic and Pacific Oceans, as well as the two continents through Costa Rica to the north and Colombia to the south. Panama is one of the prime crossroads of the world.

Panama has a tropical climate in which heat and humidity predominate. Average annual temperatures along the coasts range from 73 to 81°F (23 to 27°C), with temperatures cooling slightly as elevation increases. Although a drier season prevails from January to May, rainfall is somewhat high throughout the year, with the east coast receiving more rain than the west.

About 2.7 million people live in Panama. Mestizos make up the majority of the population, with whites accounting for about 10 percent, West Indians 14 percent, and Indians 6 percent. Spanish is the official language, but many people, particularly the educated, speak English as well. The standard of living in Panama on average is better than that of most Latin American countries. The country's infrastructure, especially in Panama City, the capital, and in and around the Canal Zone, is modern and efficient.

Economy and Taxes

Panama's economy is founded on commerce, banking and financial services, and tourism. In recent years, the country has gained prominence as an international financial center. Although tax rates on local income are high in Panama, the country's tax code provides a variety of significant incentives, including the following:

193

- Income from foreign sources is not subject to tax.
- Projects and enterprises that fall within the tourism sector are eligible for numerous incentives, including these:
  - An exemption from taxes on assets
  - An exemption from taxes on capital
  - Up to a 20-years exemption on real estate taxes
  - An exemption from income tax on the interest earned by creditors conducting business that invests in hotels
  - An exemption from income tax for 15 years if the project is located in one of nine geographical zones designated for tourist development
  - A possible reduction of 50 percent of taxable income for individuals and companies that invest in stocks or bonds issued by tourist companies

Contacts

Panama Consulate of New York
1212 Avenue of the Americas, 10th Floor
New York, NY 10036
Telephone: 212-840-2450; fax: 212-840-2469

Panama Consulate of Washington, D.C.
2862 McGill Terrace, N.W.
Washington, D.C. 20008
Telephone: 202-483-1407; fax: 202-387-6141

Panama Consulate of Miami
444 Brickell Avenue, Suite 729
Miami, FL 33131
Telephone: 305-371-7031; fax: 305-371-2907

Panama Consulate of Los Angeles
435 N. Roxbury Drive, Suite 207
Beverly Hills, CA 90210
Telephone: 310-859-7583; fax: 310-273-5339

Panama Tourist Bureau
P.O. Box 4421, Zone 5
Republic of Panama
Telephone: +507-226-7000 or +507-226-3544; fax: +507-226-
3483 or +507-226-6856

THE PHILIPPINES

The Republic of the Philippines is an archipelago consisting of some 7,000 islands, located about 750 miles (1,210 kilometers) east of Vietnam. The total area of the nation is about 115,830 square miles (about 300,000 square kilometers). The islands of the Philippines possess a tropical marine climate with average temperatures ranging between 80°F (27°C) to 94°F (34°C). Most of the islands receive an abundant amount of rainfall.

Of all the islands that make up the Philippines, 11 (Luzon, Mindanao, Samar, Negros, Palawan, Panay, Mindoro, Leyte, Cebu, Bohol, and Masbate) are the largest and are home to most of the country's population of 77 million people. Ethnic Malays account for more than 90 percent of the population. English and Pilipino (based on Tagalog) are the country's official languages. In fact, the Philippines is the third largest English-speaking nation in the world. The standard of living throughout the islands is good in the major cities but declines in quality in the outlying areas. The overall infrastructure of the whole nation is adequate but is of higher quality in the major cities.

Economy and Taxes

The economy of the Philippines focuses on several sectors, including agriculture, light industry, textiles, chemicals, electronics assembly, pharmaceuticals, wood products, and petroleum refining. In recent years, the government has enacted various incentives to promote the nation's economy and particularly its industries. The Omnibus Investment Code, for example, provides incentives to investors who engage in high-priority economic activities, and includes the following:

- A 100-percent income tax holiday of six years for pioneer companies and four years for nonpioneer companies (The holiday is extendible for two years.)
- An income tax reduction of three years for expansions
- An exemption from national or local contractor's tax

- Tax and duty-free importation of capital equipment and spare parts
- A tax credit on capital equipment obtained from local sources
- A deduction of labor expenses from taxable income

Companies that set up operations in "less developed" areas, as classified by the government, are eligible for special incentives, such as these:

- A full deduction from taxable income of the costs necessary for infrastructure and public facilities that affect the operation of the company
- A double deduction of labor expenses

The Philippines also has established export processing zones. Companies that establish operations in the zones are eligible for the following incentives:

- An exemption from local taxes
- An exemption from local licenses and fees
- An exemption from real estate taxes as applied to production equipment that is not attached to the land
- A special tax on merchandise in a zone
- An exemption from the 15 percent branch profits remittance tax

Contacts
Embassy of the Philippines
1600 Massachusetts Avenue, N.W.
Washington, D.C. 20036
Telephone: 202-467-9300; fax: 202-328-7614

Philippine Department of Tourism
556 Fifth Avenue
New York, NY 10036;
Telephone: 212-575-7915

Department of Trade and Industry
Industry and Investment Building, 4th Floor
385 Gen. Gil J. Puyat Avenue
Makati City, Republic of the Philippines
Telephone: 632-895-3515; fax: 632-896-1166

U.S. Agency for International Development (USAID)
Ramon Magsaysay Center
1680 Roxas Boulevard
Manila, Philippines
Telephone: 632-522-4411; fax: 632-521-5241

American Chamber of Commerce of the Philippines, Inc.
   (AMCHAM)
2nd Floor, Corinthian Plaza
Paseo de Roxas
Makati City, Philippines
Telephone: 632-818-7911 to 15; fax: 632-816-6359

PORTUGAL

Lying amid the trade routes that connect northern and southern Europe, Africa, North and South America, and Asia, Portugal enjoys a prime location in the western part of the Iberian Peninsula. Portugal's area, including the islands of Madeira and the Azores, is 35,553 square miles (92,082 square kilometers). The country possesses a varying topography between coastal plains and interior mountains.

Portugal's climate varies with latitude and elevation, being mostly temperate in the north and Mediterranean in the southern lowlands. Average annual temperatures range from about 50°F (10°C) in the north to around 68°F (20°C) in the south. Winters are generally mild and of short duration. The country's overall rainfall is somewhat low, with the north receiving more rain than the south.

Portugal has a population of about 10 million, with most of its people able to trace their ancestry to Iberians and Moors. Portuguese, of course, is the principal language, but many people, particularly the educated, speak English. French is common in some of the country's northern regions. Portugal's standard of living compares favorably with the levels common throughout most of Europe. Although the country's infrastructure is adequate, the government has committed some $20 billion in recent years to modernize transportation and communications systems.

Economy and Taxes

Portugal's economy has been one of Europe's leaders over the past several years. The country has also become an attractive site for investment. Between the years 1986 and 1992, for example, direct foreign investment increased from $164 million to $4.4 billion. Investment continued at impressive rates throughout the 1990s and into the new century. Portugal joined the EU in 1986, and since then the government has established programs to open the country to world trade, promote business, and encourage investment. In May 1998 Portugal became a member of the European Monetary Union, further enhancing its position in trade.

To encourage investment a variety of tax incentives is available to specific types of business, including these:

- Real estate holding companies that were incorporated during or after 1989 may be entitled to a reduced corporate tax rate of 25 percent for a period of between 7 and 10 years.
- Only 50 percent of the dividends on shares obtained during a process of privatization are subject to tax for a period of five years after the date of acquisition.
- Companies that undertake major investment projects aimed at increasing exports may be eligible for tax incentives formulated on an individual basis.

(Additional incentives are available in Madeira, which is a part of Portugal. Refer to the section on Madeira for more information on these incentives.)

Contacts

Embassy of Portugal
2125 Kalorama Road, N.W.
Washington, D.C. 20008
Telephone: 202-328-8610 or 202-328-9025; fax: 202-462-3726

Consulate General of Portugal
630 Fifth Avenue, Suite 310–378
New York, NY 10111
Telephone: 212-246-4580 or 212-765-2980; fax: 212-459-0190

Consulate General of Portugal
3298 Washington Street
San Francisco, CA 94115
Telephone: 415-921-1443; fax: 415-346-1440

Portuguese Trade Commission
590 Fifth Avenue, 3rd Floor
New York, NY 10036-4702
Telephone: 212-345-4610; fax: 212-575-4737

Portuguese National Tourist Office
590 Fifth Avenue, 4th Floor
New York, NY 10036-4704
Telephone: 212-354-4403; fax: 212-764-6137

Portuguese Trade and Tourism Office
1900 L Street, N.W., Suite 310
Washington, D.C. 20036
Telephone: 202-331-8222; fax: 202-331-8236

Portuguese Trade and Tourism Office
88 Kearny Street, Suite 1770
San Francisco, CA 941-8
Telephone: 415-391-7080; fax: 415-391-7147

PUERTO RICO

Puerto Rico is the largest island of an island group located about 950 miles (about 1,600 kilometers) southeast of Miami. The official name of the group is the Commonwealth of Puerto Rico; it is a territory of the United States, but it enjoys internal self-government.

The island of Puerto Rico is a rough rectangle with an area of about 3,500 square miles (9,100 square kilometers). Coastal lowlands rise into hills and a mountainous interior that in some places has an elevation of more than 4,000 feet (about 1,230 meters). The trade winds blowing from the east bring plentiful rainfall, and much of the island is covered with tropical rainforests. Temperatures vary little and remain warm throughout the year. Even in the highlands temperatures are relatively constant and not much cooler than the coasts.

Close to 4 million people live in Puerto Rico, with about 1.5 million living in San Juan, the capital. Puerto Rico's population is a mix of Spanish, other Europeans, Africans, and Native Americans. Together its people have created a unique and fascinating culture. Spanish and English are official languages, but Spanish is the first language for most Puerto Ricans. Spanish is also the language of business.

Puerto Rico has one of the finest standards of living in Latin America. The island infrastructure is of high quality, and its telecommunication systems are state of the art.

Economy and Taxes

Puerto Rico's economy is one of the strongest and most diverse of all the Caribbean. Its economy typically outperforms those of its neighbors, and the Puerto Rican people have the third highest per capita income in the Western Hemisphere, surpassed only by the United States and Canada. Of all Latin American nations, only Mexico and Brazil exceed Puerto Rico's total volume in external trade. Since 1993, the island's annual GDP has averaged 7 percent; in 1996 the GDP was $45.5 billion.

The island's prosperity is a direct result of far-sighted government initiatives begun in the late 1940s. Realizing that the island's economy needed to be diversified if it was to expand and remain competitive, the island government established the Economic Development Agency in 1950, its objective is to assist local and mainland investors in their efforts to establish manufacturing operations on the island. Various incentives, including tax benefits, were offered to encourage investment. Today, Puerto Rico's economic engine is fueled by manufacturing, tourism, and a vigorous service sector. Puerto Rico has also become a regional financial services center, with many major banks from the United States, Canada, and Spain, as well as numerous financial services companies, represented on the island. It has been estimated that close to $40 billion is controlled by Puerto Rican financial services firms and banks.

Puerto Rico's tax system offers a variety of incentives, including the following:

- Residents of Puerto Rico do not pay federal income taxes, except in cases in which they derive income from sources outside the island.
- Corporate profits earned in Puerto Rico receive federal tax credits after the profits are remitted to U.S. parent companies.
- Companies whose operations focus on manufacturing are eligible for an exemption of 90 percent from Puerto Rican taxes, including state taxes on corporate earnings, real estate, and personal property. These exemptions may last for a period of 10 to 25 years, depending on the location of the company.
- Service companies are eligible for an exemption of 90 percent from Puerto Rican taxes, including state taxes on corporate earnings, real estate, and personal property. These exemptions may last for a period of 10 to 25 years, depending upon the location of the company.
- Companies may be eligible for an exemption of 60 percent

on excise and other taxes required for licenses throughout the time of the tax exemption.

- Companies may defer their tax-exempt years on an annual basis.
- Companies whose operations include special projects in tourism may be eligible for specific incentives as a result of the Tourism Development Law of 1993, such as these:
  — Approved projects may receive an exemption from various taxes for a 10-year period. The exemptions may be renewed for another period of up to 10 years.
  — Income and dividends from tourism projects may be exempt from taxes at a rate of up to 90 percent. In the islands of Vieques and Culebra, the exemption may be 100 percent.
  — Approved projects may be eligible for a 50 percent tax credit in regard to investments.
- Companies operating in Puerto Rico's free-trade zones enjoy such specific incentives as these:
  — An exemption for export manufacturing
  — A tax-free and duty-free base that lies within the jurisdiction of the United States

In addition, the 1998 Tax Incentives Act provides many enhanced deductions and inducements.

- Companies new to Puerto Rico or companies already established on the island and planning to expand their operations by at least 25 percent may be eligible for the following:
  — A minimum-maximum income tax of 2 to 7 percent
  — A 200-percent deduction for research and development
  — A full-expenses deduction for investment in buildings, machinery, or equipment in the same year
  — A 200-percent deduction for job-training costs
  — Elimination of the "tollgate" tax, which is a tax at the time of distribution on dividends repatriated to the parent company

— A total exemption from real and personal property taxes during initial construction during the first year of operation and 90 percent thereafter

— Qualified companies' not being subject to tax on passive income derived from eligible investments made from industrial development income

— Manufacturers' potential eligibility for a 100-percent exemption from excise taxes on raw materials, machinery and equipment, and in some cases excise taxes on fuels

— An exemption from income tax on interest earned by financial institutions on loans up to $50,000 to small- and medium-sized companies for the purpose of expansion

Contacts

Puerto Rico Development Administration
666 Fifth Avenue, 15th Floor
New York, NY 10103
Telephone: 1-888-5-PRIDCO

Puerto Rico Economic Development Administration
233 N. Michigan Avenue
Chicago, IL 60601
Telephone: 312-565-0910

Puerto Rico Economic Development Administration
355 F.D. Roosevelt Avenue
Hato Rey
Puerto Rico 00918
Telephone: 1-888-5-PRIDCO

Puerto Rico Chamber of Commerce
P.O. Box 9024033
San Juan, PR 00902-4033
Telephone: 787-721-6060; fax: 787-723-1891

Puerto Rico Tourism Company
666 Fifth Avenue, 15th Floor
New York, NY 10103
Telephone: 1-800-866-STAR

Puerto Rico Tourism Company
901 Ponce de Leon Boulevard, Suite 101
Coral Gables, FL 33134
Telephone: 1-800-866-STAR

SAINT KITTS AND NEVIS

St. Kitts and Nevis comprise a two-island nation in the Caribbean Sea about one-third of the way from Puerto Rico to Trinidad and Tobago. Together, the islands have an area of about 102 square miles (about 269 square kilometers). The islands possess a subtropical climate in which there is little seasonal variation of temperature, which hovers around 80°F (27°C). However, rainfall varies, with a rainy season occurring between May and November.

About 44,000 people live on St. Kitts and Nevis, most descended from Africans. The islands have a long association with Great Britain, and British influence is apparent. English is the principal language, and British architecture and traditions are common. St. Kitts and Nevis have a solid infrastructure and offer a high quality of life.

Economy and Taxes

The economy of St. Kitts and Nevis center around tourism, light manufacturing, agriculture, and a vibrant financial services sector that has played an increasingly greater role in the islands' prosperity.

Although St. Kitts and Nevis created the only International Financial Center in the Caribbean in April 1997, the financial services sector has grown rapidly. The banks and companies that make up the sector complement the offshore trust services centered on Nevis.

When the Island Assembly of Nevis adopted the Nevis International Trust Ordinance in 1994, it created one of the most flexible and comprehensive asset protection trust (APT) laws in the world. The Nevis APT rapidly gained popularity among international investors because of the excellent protection it provides. A Nevis trust places personal assets out of the reach of foreign governments and their agencies, creditors, litigious plaintiffs, and lawyers. The law is quite clear in its application. Nevis judges will not recognize any nondomestic court orders regarding any APT established in Nevis. Any foreign creditor or agency must try its suit through the courts of Nevis, regardless of any previous legal actions or judgments. In addition, anyone bringing a suit against an APT established in Nevis must first post a bond of U.S.$25,000 with the government that will be applied as necessary to court and other costs. Further, the statute of limitations for filing a legal challenge to an APT established in Nevis runs out a year from the date of the creation of the trust. On top of all this, the burden of proof is carried by the foreign claimant, especially in cases where fraudulent intent of the trust or on the part of its officers or beneficiaries is claimed.

Along with its asset protection, Nevis APTs permit the same individual to serve as creator, beneficiary, and protector of the trust. This goes well beyond the trust laws of most jurisdictions and gives an individual significant control over his assets.

APTs also provide privacy. Trust documents are not required to be filed with the Nevis government and thus do not appear in the public record, ensuring confidentiality. The only information required to establish an APT on Nevis is a simple document identifying the trustee, the date the trust is established, the date of filing, and the name of the local trust company that represents the APT. A filing fee of U.S.$200 is necessary, as is an annual fee of U.S.$200 for maintenance.

In addition to the benefits of APTs on Nevis, St. Kitts and Nevis also offer major tax incentives, including these:

- There are no personal income taxes in St. Kitts and Nevis.
- The islands have no sales taxes.
- The islands have no gift taxes.
- The islands have no estate duties.
- Corporate tax holidays from 10 to 15 years are available for eligible companies.
- Companies that produce goods exclusively for export outside the CARICOM region may be eligible for a tax holiday of up to 15 years. (Upon conclusion of the tax holiday,

a further tax concession in the form of a rebate of a portion of the income tax paid, based on export profits as a percentage of total profits, may be available. This rebate may range from 25 to 50 percent.

- Companies may be eligible for an exemption from import duties on raw materials, parts, and production supplies.
- Owners of hotels of more than 30 bedrooms may be exempt from income tax for a period of 10 years. Owners of hotels of fewer than 30 bedrooms may qualify for an exemption of tax on profits for five years.

Contacts

Consulate of St. Kitts and Nevis
Economic Affairs Division
414 E. 75th Street
New York, NY 10021
Telephone: 212-535-1234; fax: 212-535-6854

Ministry of Trade and Industry
P.O. Box 600
Church Street
Basseterre, St. Kitts
West Indies
Telephone: +1-869-465-2302; fax: +1-869-465-1778

Embassy of St. Kitts and Nevis
3216 New Mexico Avenue, N.W.
Washington, D.C. 20016
Telephone: 202-686-2636; fax: 202-686-5740

Department of Tourism, St. Kitts and Nevis
Pelican Mall, Bay Rd.
P.O. Box 132
Basseterre, St. Kitts
West Indies
Telephone: +1-869-465-2620/4040; fax: +1-869-465-8794

Nevis Tourism Bureau
Main Street
Charlestown, Nevis
West Indies
Telephone: +1-869-469-1042; fax: +1-869-469-1066

St. Kitts and Nevis Tourism Office
365 Bay Street, Suite 806
Toronto, Ontario M5H 2V1
Canada
Telephone: 416-368-6707; fax: 416-368-3934

SEYCHELLES

Seychelles lies in the Indian Ocean, northeast of Madagascar. The country consists of some 118 islands that have an overall area of about 145 square miles (375 square kilometers). The islands possess a tropical marine climate with an average annual temperature of about 75°F (24°C) with little seasonal variation. Rainfall varies among the islands, but in general they all receive generous precipitation.

About 79,000 people live in Seychelles, most of whom have descended from Asians, Africans, and Europeans. English and French are official languages; however, Creole, mostly based on French but including much of the many languages once spoken on the islands, is also common. The standard of living in the capital, Victoria, is good, but the quality of life in some of the outlying areas is not likely to satisfy modern expectations. The infrastructure on the islands is considered to be reliable and among the best of the region.

Economy and Taxes

Seychelles has become a prime tourist site in the Eastern Hemisphere, with more than 100,000 people visiting the islands annually. Realizing that expansion of the economy depends on more than just tourism, the island government has initiated various programs to attract investment. Seychelles offers numerous tax incentives, including these:

- No income tax
- No withholding tax on dividends
- No wealth or gift taxes
- No property tax
- No taxes on properties
- No tax on capital gains
- No death duties

In 1994 the government enacted the Investment Promotion

Act to encourage business investment in Seychelles. The act provides the following incentives:

- There is a low business tax rate of 15 percent with further tax credits possible; an effective rate of 9 percent is possible.
- There are no import duties on capital equipment.
- Accelerated depreciation schedules of up to 150 percent of the original cost of assets are available for certain categories of investments.
- A tax holiday is available for certain companies.
- Companies that obtain a license under the International Trade Zone Act are exempt from all taxes provided their operations and output are intended for the export market.
- Any changes in taxation after the issue of a certificate of approval cannot be detrimental to the company in question.

Seychelles has also positioned itself as a center for the establishment of international trusts. The trust law of Seychelles has many notable features, such as the following:

- The transfer or disposition by an individual who creates an international trust cannot be invalidated by a foreign rule of forced heirship.
- The accumulation of income is not restricted.
- Settlors or trustees can be named as beneficiaries under the trust.
- The settlor chooses the law governing an international trust, and this law is the proper law; the choice may be express or implied in the terms of the trust.
- Confidentiality is maintained. Under the trust law, it is prohibited to disclose or produce any information relating to an international trust, except under an injunction of the Seychelles Supreme Court as a result of an application made by the Seychelles attorney-general. Such applications may be made only in inquiry or trial in relation to the trafficking of narcotics and dangerous drugs, arms trafficking or money laundering.

- There is no requirement to mention the names of the settlor or the name of beneficiary unless the latter is a Seychellois national or a body corporate resident in Seychelles.
- A one-time registration fee of U.S. $100 is required.

Contacts

Embassy of Seychelles
820 Second Avenue, Suite 900 F
New York, NY 10017
Telephone: 212-687-9766; fax: 212-922-9177

Seychelles Department of Tourism and Transport
Independence House, Victoria
P.O. Box 92
Mahe, Seychelles
Telephone: 248-225313, 224030; fax: 248-224035, 225131

SINGAPORE

The Republic of Singapore is located at the southern tip of the Malay Peninsula. Its position is at the heart of the international trade routes and makes Singapore one of the most important gateways to Asia. Singapore consists of about 50 small islands with a total area of about 224 square miles (580 square kilometers), making the nation smaller than New York City. Singapore is the largest of the islands and home to the capital city, also named Singapore.

Singapore has a tropical climate with an average annual temperature of 81°F (27°C). There is little variation in temperature throughout the year, and although rainfall is relatively consistent, November to January are the wettest months.

About 3.5 million people live in Singapore. About 77 percent of the population is Chinese, and Malays and Indians make up most of the rest. Because the country is a center of international business, several languages are spoken, the most common being Chinese, Malay, Tamil, and English, which is the language of government and much international business. Singapore's residents and visitors enjoy one of the highest standards of living in Asia. The city of Singapore is considered by many to be among the world's cleanest and safest.

Economy and Taxes

Singapore's diversified economy is one of the strongest of the Far East. Numerous sectors are vital to the economy, including electronics, pharmaceuticals, chemicals, machinery, plastics, steel, clothing, processed foods, timber products, rubber products, shipbuilding, and oil refining. Global shipping services center on Singapore's deep-water port, which is one of the best and busiest in the region. Financial and business services have gained importance in recent years, making Singapore a trade and finance center.

To promote the economy, the government of Singapore has enacted various incentives to encourage investment on the part of individuals (particularly nonresidents) and businesses.

The following tax incentives are aimed at nonresident individuals:

- Nonresidents who remain in Singapore for not more than 60 days in a year are not subject to tax.
- Nonresidents who remain in Singapore for more than 60 but less than 183 days in a year are subject to tax on income from or received in Singapore at a rate applicable to Singapore residents or 15 percent, whichever is greater.
- Nonresidents who remain in Singapore for more than 183 days in a year are considered residents and are taxed at a rate calculated on a sliding scale ranging from 2 percent on the first $5,000 to 28 percent on income greater than $400,000.

The following incentives are aimed at businesses. Most business incentives are offered under the Economic Expansion Incentives Act and are administered by the Economic Development Board, the Trade Development Board, the Monetary Authority of Singapore, and the Ministry of Finance. The most important of these incentives include these:

- Manufacturing and high-tech services are eligible for pioneer tax holidays of up to 10 years. Qualifying enterprises may be eligible for tax reduction for another 10 years.
- Investment allowances of up to 50 percent are available.
- Financial services enjoy a reduced tax rate.
- Oil traders, international traders, and shippers may qualify for a reduced rate on offshore business.

Contacts

Singapore Economic Development Board
55 E. 59th Street
New York, NY 10022-11122
Telephone: 212-421-2200; fax: 212-421-2206

Singapore Economic Development Board
180 N. Stetson Avenue, Suite 970
Chicago, IL 60601-6712
Telephone: 312-565-1100; fax: 312-565-1994

Singapore Economic Development Board
1100 New York Avenue, N.W., Suite 440
Washington, D.C. 20005-1701
Telephone: 202-223-2570; fax: 202-223-2571

Singapore Economic Development Board
210 Twin Dolphin Drive
Redwood City, CA 94065-1402
Telephone: 650-591-9102; fax: 650-591-1328

Consulate of the Republic of Singapore
231 E. 51st Street
New York, NY 10022
Telephone: 212-223-3331; fax: 212-826-5028

Consulate of the Republic of Singapore
1670 Pine Street
San Francisco, CA 94109
Telephone: 415-928-8508; fax: 415-673-0083

TURKS AND CAICOS

The Turks and Caicos are two island groups southeast of the Bahamas. The Turks consist of Grand Turk, Salt Cay, and several uninhabited cays, while the Caicos include Grand Caicos and five other islands. The overall area of the islands is about 165 square miles (430 square kilometers). The Turks and Caicos enjoy a tropical marine climate with abundant sunshine, and average annual temperatures of about 85°F (29°C).

About 16,300 people live on the islands, which make up a British dependency. Although most of the residents are of African or mixed descent, English is the official language and British influence is pronounced. The British have maintained a modern infrastructure and telecommunications system, and the standard of living on the islands is high.

Economy and Taxes

Tourism and offshore financial services are the principal sectors of the islands' economy. In a program to encourage investment, the government offers such numerous tax incentives as the following:

- No income tax in the islands
- No tax on capital gains
- No tax on corporate dividends
- No withholding tax
- No tax on property
- No value-added tax
- No sales tax
- No taxes on estates, inheritances, gifts, or successions
- No exchange controls

Contacts

TCIvest
Chief Executive Officer
Hibiscus Square, Pond Street
P.O. Box 105
Grand Turk
Telephone: 649-94-62058/2852; fax: 649-94-61464

Turks and Caicos Islands Tourist Board
11645 Biscayne Boulevard, Suite 302
North Miami, FL 33181
Telephone: 305-891-4117 or 800-241-0824; fax: 305-891-7096

UNITED KINGDOM

The United Kingdom, commonly called Great Britain (or sometimes simply England), includes the island of Great Britain (shared by England, Scotland, and Wales) and the northern one-sixth of the island of Ireland. The overall area of the United Kingdom is 94,525 square miles (244,820 square kilometers). The topography of Great Britain consists mostly of rugged hills and low mountains in the north and plains in the east and southeast.

The islands of England and Ireland have temperate climates with milder temperatures than one would expect at their latitude. Average annual temperatures range between 52°F (about 11°C) in the south and 48°F (about 9°C) in the north. Few extremes in temperatures are the norm. With winds typically blowing in from the Atlantic, fog, mist, and clouds are more common than sunshine.

The population of the United Kingdom is almost 59 million. More than 80 percent of the people are English, with Scots, Irish, Welsh, and various other minority groups comprising the remainder. The people of the United Kingdom enjoy a fully modern infrastructure and excellent standard of living.

Economy and Taxes

The United Kingdom is one of the world's great commercial and financial centers. Its diversified economy is now the fourth largest in the world.

Although the United Kingdom does not offer tax incentives as many tax havens do, in the British tax code is the phrase "resident but not domiciled." The phrase bestows special tax status under specific conditions. What it means is that individuals can live in England and therefore be residents but not be domiciled there, meaning that they do not maintain a permanent home in Great Britain. Such individuals can maintain a permanent home in another country but reside, or live, in Britain. Individuals who are "resident but not domiciled" are required to pay tax only on income that is actually brought into the United Kingdom. Consequently, under British tax law an individual can accumulate income earned abroad in offshore accounts and not be taxed on these funds.

A note of caution is necessary here. Because the strategy is somewhat complex, individuals considering taking advantage of the "resident but not domiciled" provision are advised to consult a tax advisor experienced with British tax law, particularly in regard to the residency issue.

Contacts

British Consulate
845 Third Avenue
New York, NY 10022
Telephone: 212-745-0200 or 212-745-0495; fax: 212-745-3062 or
    212-745-0456

British Consulate
Federal Reserve Plaza, 25th Floor
600 Atlantic Avenue
Boston, MA 02210
Telephone: 617-248-9555; fax: 617-248-9578

British Consulate
The Wrigley Building, 13th Floor
400 N. Michigan Avenue
Chicago, IL 60611
Telephone: 312-346-1810; fax: 312-464-0661

British Consulate
245 Peachtree Center Avenue, Suite 2700
Marquis 1 Tower, 27th Floor
Atlanta, GA 30303
Telephone: 404-524-5856; fax: 404-524-3153

British Consulate
11766 Wilshire Boulevard, Suite 400
Los Angeles, CA 90025
Telephone: 310-477-3322; fax: 310-575-1450

USING OFFSHORE HAVENS FOR PRIVACY AND PROFIT

USING OFFSHORE HAVENS FOR PRIVACY AND PROFIT

ADAM STARCHILD

PALADIN PRESS • BOULDER, COLORADO

Also by Adam Starchild:

Keep What You Own: Protect Your Money, Property, and Family
    from Courts, Creditors, and the IRS
Protect Your Assets: How to Avoid Falling Victim to the
    Government's Forfeiture Laws
Swiss Money Secrets: How You Can Legally Hide Your
    Money in Switzerland

Using Offshore Havens for Privacy and Profit, Revised and Updated
by Adam Starchild

Copyright © 2001 by Adam Starchild

ISBN 10: 1-58160-280-4
ISBN 13: 978-1-58160-280-7
Printed in the United States of America

Published by Paladin Press, a division of
Paladin Enterprises, Inc.
Gunbarrel Tech Center
7077 Winchester Circle
Boulder, Colorado 80301 USA
+1.303.443.7250

Direct inquiries and/or orders to the above address.

Visit our Web site at www.paladin-press.com